Midwest Living®

TASTE OF THE SEASONS

Meredith® Consumer Marketing
Des Moines, Iowa

Midwest Living® Taste of the Seasons

Meredith® Corporation Consumer Marketing
VICE PRESIDENT, CONSUMER MARKETING: Janet Donnelly
CONSUMER PRODUCT MARKETING DIRECTOR: Heather Sorensen
BUSINESS DIRECTOR: Ron Clingman
CONSUMER MARKETING PRODUCT MANAGER: Wendy Merical
SENIOR PRODUCTION MANAGER: Al Rodruck

Waterbury Publications, Inc.
EDITORIAL DIRECTOR: Lisa Kingsley
ASSOCIATE EDITORS: Tricia Bergman, Mary Williams
CREATIVE DIRECTOR: Ken Carlson
ASSOCIATE DESIGN DIRECTOR: Doug Samuelson
PRODUCTION ASSISTANT: Mindy Samuelson
CONTRIBUTING COPY EDITORS: Terri Fredrickson, Peg Smith
CONTRIBUTING INDEXER: Elizabeth T. Parson

***Midwest Living*® Magazine**
EDITOR IN CHIEF: Greg Philby
CREATIVE DIRECTOR: Geri Wolfe Boesen
EXECUTIVE EDITOR: Trevor Meers
FOOD EDITOR: Hannah Agran
COPY CHIEF: Maria Duryée

Meredith National Media Group
PRESIDENT: Tom Harty

Meredith Corporation
PRESIDENT AND CHIEF EXECUTIVE OFFICER: Stephen M. Lacy

IN MEMORIAM: E.T. Meredith III (1933–2003)

Pictured on the front cover:
Spiced Pear-Cranberry Cobbler
(recipe on page 176)
Photographer: Kritsada

Contents

How a Season Should Taste

CERTAIN DAYS JUST SEEM TO LIFT UP WITH A CERTAIN FLAVOR IN THE AIR.
It's as though the whole day exists just to articulate that one food, that one delectable taste, that is perfect at this particular moment. The day and the food are inseparable.

You know the feeling. We can, and do, have our favorite foods that we think of often. But these are the seasonal ones, the ones that we await with great anticipation until they crop up to our delight.

For me, each spring will bring a rhubarb day, a day that from morning until night, I am consumed with the need to taste a crisp, sour stalk of springtime, even if the rhubarb may be no more than a wrinkled shoot just pluming out of the muddy thawing ground. It happens when it happens, and when it does, it comes with ferocity and nothing else will satisfy. At least, until, say, morel mushroom season kicks in or the first strawberries begin to blush.

Then come farmers markets and fresh beans and peas... sweet corn season... fresh fish... apples... cold-weather casseroles. Our calendars are defined by our plates.

Living in the Midwest, where seasons are so pure and pronounced, this is not a surprise. It's a celebration. With more than 20 years of publishing *Midwest Living* ideas, we know well the compelling foods and flavors that embody the seasons. In this first collection of *Taste of the Seasons*, we package the wonderful flavors that we have accumulated during the past year, all tested by our Test Kitchen for easy, reliable preparation, and all tasted by us to be perfectly suited to how a Midwest season should taste.

Happy cooking.

Greg Philby
Editor in Chief

FINGERLING POTATO
SALAD WITH HONEY-
THYME VINAIGRETTE,
PAGE 30

Spring

BREAKFAST
Morel-Zucchini Frittata 8

BREADS
Honey Cream Scones 11

Honey-Rhubarb Muffins 11

Kansas Zwiebach 8

BEVERAGES
Shamrock Smoothies 13

MAIN DISHES
Chicken Chowder with Dilly Dumplings 14

Chicken Enchiladas Adobo 24

Cranberry-Stuffed Chicken Burgers 23

Golden Trout 29

Grilled Steaks with Morel and Caramelized Onion Sauce 13

Herbed Oven-Fried Chicken 20

Lemon-Rosemary Chicken with Roasted Vegetables 19

Salmon-Asparagus Pasta 29

Smoked Trout Cakes 29

Turkey with Creamy Morel Sauce 26

SIDES
Crispened New Potatoes 35

Crunchy Asian Noodle Slaw 32

Dutch Lettuce 30

Fingerling Potato Salad with Honey-Thyme Vinaigrette 30

Morel and Potato au Gratin 35

Nutty Apple-Cherry Slaw 32

Oven-Roasted Asparagus with Lemon-Chive Butter 34

Sugar Snap Peas with Sesame Seeds 34

SWEETS
Caramel and Chocolate Kettle Corn Crispie Bars 51

Go-Anywhere Rhubarb Squares 51

Honey-Rosemary Shortbread Cookies 48

Indiana Sugar Cream Pie 39

Maple Syrup Cake 44

Missouri Gooey Butter Cake 43

Rhubarb Cheesecake 47

Rhubarb Custard Pie 40

Rhubarb-Lemon Chiffon Pie 40

Strawberry-Coconut Thumbprints 48

Morel-Zucchini Frittata

A generous amount of morels dresses up this Italian cousin of the omelet.

START TO FINISH 45 minutes

    4 ounces fresh morels or other mushrooms,
      or 1 ounce dried morels, reconstituted*
    ½ cup chopped zucchini
    1 tablespoon chopped onion
    1 tablespoon chopped green sweet pepper
    2 tablespoons butter
    6 eggs
    ¼ cup milk
    ¼ teaspoon salt
      Pepper
      Tomato wedges
      Parsley sprigs

1. In a 10-inch ovenproof skillet, cook morels (cut large ones into bite-size strips), zucchini, onion and sweet pepper in butter until zucchini is tender and most of the liquid is evaporated.

2. In a mixing bowl, beat eggs with milk, salt and pepper to taste; pour over vegetable mixture in skillet. Cook over medium-low heat, lifting edges occasionally. Cook about 4 minutes or until edges begin to set and the underside is lightly browned.

3. Place pan under broiler, 4 to 5 inches from heat. Broil about 2 minutes or just until set. Loosen sides and bottom of frittata with a spatula. Serve immediately from skillet or slide frittata, face up, onto a warm serving platter. Garnish with tomato wedges and parsley. **Makes 3 servings.**

*Note: To reconstitute mushrooms, cover dried morels with warm water. Let stand for 45 minutes; drain.

Per serving: 255 cal, 19 g fat, 449 mg chol, 419 mg sodium, 6 g carbo, 1 g fiber, 15 g pro.

Kansas Zwiebach

When Mennonites came to Kansas, they brought their German language, Turkey Red wheat and the recipe for this addictively sweet soft dinner roll with a doughy topknot. The secret to its rich taste and moistness: potato water, sugar, butter and egg. Don't confuse it with the tooth-breaking cracker of the same name.

PREP 50 minutes   **RISE** 1 hour 20 minutes   **STAND** 20 minutes   **BAKE** 18 minutes

    ½ cup warm potato cooking water or water
      (105° to 115°)
    ¼ cup sugar
    1 package active dry yeast
    1 cup milk
    ¾ cup butter
    1 teaspoon salt
    5¼ to 5¾ cups all-purpose flour
    1 egg

1. In a small bowl, combine potato water, sugar and yeast. Let stand about 10 minutes or until yeast is dissolved. Meanwhile, in a small saucepan, combine milk, butter and salt. Heat and stir just until warm (120° to 130°) and butter is almost melted.

2. In a large mixing bowl, combine butter mixture and 2 cups of the flour. Add the yeast mixture and egg. Beat with an electric mixer on low to medium speed for 30 seconds, scraping sides of bowl constantly. Beat on high speed for 3 minutes. Using a wooden spoon, stir in as much of the remaining flour as you can.

3. Turn dough out onto a lightly floured surface. Knead in enough of the remaining flour to make a moderately soft dough that is smooth and elastic (3 to 5 minutes total). Shape dough into a ball. Place in a lightly greased bowl, turning once to grease surface. Cover and let rise in a warm place until double in size (about 1 hour).

4. Punch dough down. Turn out onto a lightly floured surface. Cover and let rest for 10 minutes. Lightly grease a very large (or two medium) baking sheet(s); set aside.

5. For each zwiebach, pinch off enough dough to make a 1½-inch ball, gently pulling dough and tucking edges under to create a smooth top. Place dough ball on prepared baking sheet. Pinch off enough dough to make a 1-inch ball; place on top of larger ball. Using a lightly floured finger, press down firmly into center of the ball. Cover shaped rolls and let stand in a warm place for 20 minutes.

6. Bake in a 350° oven for 18 to 20 minutes or until golden brown. Remove from baking sheet; cool slightly on wire racks. Serve warm. **Makes about 20 rolls.**

Per roll: 201 cal, 8 g fat, 30 mg chol, 175 mg sodium, 28 g carbo, 1 g fiber, 4 g pro.

KANSAS ZWIEBACH

HONEY CREAM
SCONES

Honey Cream Scones

PREP 30 minutes **BAKE** 12 minutes

2¼ cups all-purpose flour
¼ cup cornmeal
1 tablespoon baking powder
1½ teaspoons finely shredded lemon or
    lime peel
½ teaspoon snipped fresh thyme
½ teaspoon salt
⅓ cup butter (no substitutes)
2 eggs, lightly beaten
¾ cup whipping cream, plus additional
    for brushing
⅓ cup honey
    Honey
    Edible flowers or sprigs of fresh thyme
    (optional)

1. In a large bowl, combine flour, cornmeal, baking powder, lemon peel, ½ teaspoon thyme and salt. Using a pastry blender, cut in butter until mixture resembles coarse crumbs. Make a well in center of the flour mixture; set mixture aside.

2. In a medium bowl, combine eggs, whipping cream and the ⅓ cup honey. Add egg mixture all at once to flour mixture. Using a fork, stir just until moistened. (Dough will be very sticky.)

3. Turn dough out onto a well-floured surface. Knead dough by folding and pressing it for six to eight strokes or until dough is nearly smooth. Pat or lightly roll dough into an 8-inch circle about 1 inch thick. Cut into 12 wedges. Place wedges 2 inches apart on a large ungreased baking sheet. Brush with additional whipping cream.

4. Bake in a 400° oven for 12 to 15 minutes or until golden brown. Remove scones from baking sheet to a serving plate. Drizzle a little additional honey over each wedge before serving. If you like, garnish with edible flowers. Serve warm. **Makes 12 scones.**

Per scone: 249 cal, 12 g fat, 71 mg chol, 243 mg sodium, 32 g carbo, 1 g fiber, 4 g pro.

Honey-Rhubarb Muffins

The lemon-flavor honey butter accents the tart-sweet flavor of the rhubarb in these muffins.

PREP 20 minutes **BAKE** 35 minutes

1 tablespoon butter
½ cup granulated sugar
1 egg, slightly beaten
1 cup packed brown sugar
⅔ cup cooking oil
½ cup honey
½ teaspoon vanilla
2½ cups all-purpose flour
1 teaspoon baking soda
½ teaspoon salt
¾ cup sour milk*
1½ cups chopped fresh or frozen rhubarb
½ cup chopped nuts
1 recipe Whipped Honey Butter (recipe
    follows)

1. For topping: In a small bowl, cut butter into granulated sugar until mixture resembles coarse crumbs; set aside.

2. For muffins: Line muffin cups with paper bake cups; set aside. In a large mixing bowl, combine egg, brown sugar, oil, honey and vanilla.

3. In another bowl, stir together the flour, baking soda and salt. Add dry ingredients to the egg mixture alternately with sour milk, stirring after each addition until moistened (batter should be lumpy). Gently fold in the chopped rhubarb and the chopped nuts.

4. Fill muffin cups two-thirds full with batter. Sprinkle with topping. Bake in a 325° oven for 35 to 40 minutes or until golden. Remove from pans. Serve warm or cool with Whipped Honey Butter. **Makes about 21 muffins.**

*Note: To make sour milk, place 1 tablespoon white vinegar in glass measure. Add enough milk to equal ¾ cup.

Whipped Honey Butter: In a small mixing bowl, combine ½ cup softened butter and ¼ teaspoon finely shredded lemon peel. Gradually add ¼ cup honey, beating with an electric mixer on high speed until fluffy. Store, covered, in the refrigerator. Let honey butter stand at room temperature for about 1 hour before serving.

Per muffin: 270 cal, 14 g fat, 24 mg chol, 172 mg sodium, 35 g carbo, 1 g fiber, 3 g pro.

There are more than 300 varieties of honey in the United States, and every one keeps for years in your pantry.

SHAMROCK
SMOOTHIES

Shamrock Smoothies

Whip up these as a healthful alternative to the minty green shakes that arrive each spring at a certain fast-food restaurant. You can omit the rum for a fruity, colorful, alcohol-free drink.

PREP 20 minutes **FREEZE** 2 hours

    6 kiwifruit, peeled and quartered
    1 banana, peeled and cut into 1-inch pieces
    1 cup seedless green grapes
    1 ounce carton Key lime- or vanilla-flavor
        yogurt
    1 cup orange juice or white grape juice,
        well chilled
    3 tablespoons honey
    2 to 4 tablespoons rum
    1 to 2 drops green food coloring (optional)
        Fresh kiwifruit slices

1. Place kiwifruit and banana in a 15x10x1-inch baking pan. Place in freezer, uncovered, for 2 hours or until frozen.

2. In a blender, combine grapes, yogurt, orange juice, honey, rum and about one-third of the frozen fruit. Cover and blend until almost smooth. Gradually add remaining fruit, blending after each addition until almost smooth. Add food coloring, if you like.

3. Pour into glasses and garnish with kiwifruit slices. **Makes 5 (8 ounce) servings.**

Per serving: 215 cal, 1 g fat, 1 mg chol, 25 mg sodium, 48 g carbo, 4 g fiber, 4 g pro.

Grilled Steaks with Morel and Caramelized Onion Sauce

To clean fresh morels, rinse them for several minutes in a pitcher tilted under a running faucet so it overspills. Gently pat the morels dry with paper towels.

PREP 25 minutes **COOK** 18 minutes **GRILL** 18 minutes

    4 ounces fresh morel mushrooms* or other
        fresh mushrooms
    4 beef tenderloin steaks, cut 1¼ to
        1½ inches thick, or 4 boneless pork loin
        chops, cut 1¼ to 1½ inches thick
    3 tablespoons butter
    1 tablespoon brown sugar
 1½ cups coarsely chopped onions
    4 large shallots, thinly sliced (½ cup)
    2 tablespoons dry white wine, white wine
        vinegar or balsamic vinegar
    2 tablespoons snipped mixed fresh herbs
        (such as basil, sage, marjoram and savory)
    ½ teaspoon salt
    ¼ teaspoon freshly ground black pepper
    ½ cup dairy sour cream
    ¼ cup half-and-half or light cream
    1 tablespoon all-purpose flour

1. Clean morel mushrooms. Wash other mushrooms by gently wiping with a damp towel or paper towel. Trim stem ends, if necessary. Slice mushrooms (should measure ½ cup). Set aside.

2. For beef tenderloin: Grill steaks on the rack of an uncovered grill directly over medium coals until desired doneness, turning once halfway through grilling. (Allow 15 to 19 minutes for medium-rare or until an instant-read thermometer registers 145° when inserted in the center or 18 to 23 minutes for medium or 160° in the center.) For pork chops, grill chops on the rack of an uncovered grill directly over medium coals for 17 to 21 minutes or until 160° in the center, turning once halfway through grilling.

3. In a medium saucepan, melt butter over medium heat. Stir sugar into the melted butter. Add the onions and shallots. Cook, stirring frequently, about 15 minutes or until vegetables are very tender and golden brown. Stir in mushrooms, wine, herbs, salt and pepper. Cook and stir for 2 minutes more. In a small bowl, stir together sour cream, half-and-half and flour. Add to mushroom mixture. Cook and stir until bubbly. Cook and stir for 1 minute more.

4. To serve, spoon some sour cream sauce over meat; pass remaining sauce. **Makes 4 servings.**

*Note: If fresh morels aren't available, substitute 1 ounce (about ¾ cup) dried morel or porcini mushrooms. In a small bowl, cover the dried mushrooms with hot water. Let stand for 20 minutes. Rinse under warm running water; squeeze out excess moisture. Slice the mushrooms into rings.

Per serving: 439 cal, 27 g fat, 112 mg chol, 486 mg sodium, 16 g carbo, 1 g fiber, 33 g pro.

Chicken Chowder with Dilly Dumplings

This comforting chowder topped with fluffy dumplings looks and tastes like it takes all day to make, but it can be on the table in just 40 minutes. Round out the meal with a crisp green salad.

START TO FINISH 40 minutes

1 tablespoon vegetable oil
1 pound skinless, boneless chicken thighs, cut into 1-inch pieces
1 cup all-purpose flour
1 teaspoon baking powder
½ teaspoon kosher salt or ¼ teaspoon salt
2 tablespoons shortening
1 tablespoon snipped fresh chives
2 teaspoons snipped fresh dill or ¾ teaspoon dried dillweed
¼ cup plain yogurt
¼ cup milk
3 cups reduced-sodium chicken broth
1 cup sliced leeks or chopped onion
1 cup chopped carrots
1 cup frozen whole kernel corn
1 teaspoon snipped fresh dill or ½ teaspoon dried dillweed
2 tablespoons all-purpose flour
½ cup half-and-half or light cream

1. In a large saucepan, cook chicken in hot oil over medium heat until chicken is browned and no longer pink. With a slotted spoon, remove chicken from saucepan; set aside. Drain fat from saucepan.

2. Meanwhile, for dumplings, in a medium bowl, combine the 1 cup flour, the baking powder and half of the salt. Cut in shortening until mixture resembles coarse crumbs. Stir in chives and the 2 teaspoons dill. Add yogurt and milk, stirring just until moistened; set aside.

3. In the same saucepan, combine broth, leeks, carrots, frozen corn, the 1 teaspoon dill and the remaining salt. Bring to boiling; reduce heat. Drop dumpling batter into simmering liquid, making eight mounds. Return to a gentle boil; reduce heat. Simmer, covered, for 12 to 15 minutes or until a wooden toothpick inserted into dumplings comes out clean. Do not lift lid while simmering. With a slotted spoon, transfer dumplings to a platter.

4. Stir chicken into mixture in saucepan. Stir the 2 tablespoons flour into half-and-half; stir into the chicken mixture in saucepan. Cook and stir over medium heat until chowder is thickened and bubbly. Cook and stir for 1 minute more.

5. To serve, ladle chowder into four soup bowls. Top each serving with two dumplings. **Makes 4 servings.**

Per serving: 479 cal, 19 g fat, 107 mg chol, 914 mg sodium, 46 g carbo, 3 g fiber, 32 g pro.

A carpet of blue-eyed Mary wildflowers covers the floor of the woods at Giant City State Park, nestled in the Shawnee National Forest near Carbondale, Illinois. In spring, Midwestern woods yield abundant blooms, elusive morel mushrooms, and refreshing solitude.

Lemon-Rosemary Chicken with Roasted Vegetables

Few things are more enticing—and comforting—than a roast chicken crackling in the oven. The garlic, which turns creamy and mildly sweet after roasting, is absolutely delicious smeared on bites of chicken.

PREP 30 minutes **ROAST** 1 hour 15 minutes **STAND** 10 minutes

  1 pound small Yukon gold potatoes, peeled and quartered
  1 pound sweet potatoes, peeled and cut into chunks
  1 cup packaged peeled fresh baby carrots
  ¾ cup halved shallots and/or onion chunks
  ¼ cup butter, melted
  ½ teaspoon kosher salt or ¼ teaspoon salt
  ½ teaspoon ground black pepper
  1 3½- to 4-pound whole roasting chicken
  1 teaspoon finely shredded lemon peel (set aside)
  1 lemon, halved
  1 tablespoon snipped fresh parsley
  1 tablespoon snipped fresh rosemary or 1 teaspoon dried rosemary, crushed
  1 tablespoon snipped fresh thyme or 1 teaspoon dried thyme, crushed
  2 cloves garlic, minced
    Fresh thyme sprigs (optional)
    Garlic bulbs, tops sliced off (optional)
    Lemon halves (optional)

1. In a large bowl, combine Yukon gold potatoes, sweet potatoes, carrots and shallots. Drizzle vegetables with half of the melted butter. Sprinkle with half of the salt and half of the pepper; toss gently to coat.

2. Rinse the chicken body cavity; pat dry with paper towels. Skewer neck skin of chicken to back. Place the one halved lemon in body cavity. Tie legs to tail. Twist wing tips under back. Place chicken, breast side up, on a rack in a shallow roasting pan. Brush chicken with the remaining melted butter.

3. In a small bowl, stir together lemon peel, parsley, rosemary, thyme, minced garlic, the remaining salt and the remaining pepper; rub onto chicken. If you like, insert an oven-safe meat thermometer into center of an inside thigh muscle. (The thermometer should not touch bone.) Place vegetables around chicken. If you like, add fresh thyme sprigs, garlic bulbs and additional lemon halves.

4. Roast, uncovered, in a 375° oven for 1¼ to 1½ hours or until drumsticks move easily in their sockets and chicken is no longer pink (180°), stirring vegetables once or twice. Remove chicken and vegetables from oven. Cover; let stand for 10 minutes before carving chicken. (If vegetables are not done, return them to the oven while the chicken stands.) **Makes 4 to 5 servings.**

Per serving: 901 cal, 53 g fat, 233 mg chol, 605 mg sodium, 52 g carbo, 9 g fiber, 55 g pro.

Herbed Oven-Fried Chicken

Soaking the chicken in buttermilk before baking it accomplishes a couple of things. Buttermilk is acidic, so it tenderizes the meat. It also helps infuse the meat with moisture so it stays juicy.

PREP 25 minutes **MARINATE** 4 to 24 hours **BAKE** 30 minutes

4 skinless, boneless chicken breast halves (1½ pounds total)
1 cup buttermilk
½ teaspoon kosher salt or ¼ teaspoon salt
1 egg, lightly beaten
3 tablespoons water
1¼ cups panko (Japanese bread crumbs) or fine dry bread crumbs
¾ teaspoon ground sage
½ teaspoon dried thyme, crushed
¼ teaspoon dried savory, crushed
⅛ teaspoon ground black pepper

1. Place chicken in a resealable plastic bag set in a bowl.

2. For marinade: In a small bowl, stir together buttermilk and half of the salt. Pour over chicken. Seal bag; turn to coat chicken. Marinate in the refrigerator for 4 to 24 hours, turning bag occasionally.

3. Grease a 15x10x1-inch baking pan. In a small bowl, combine egg and the water. In a shallow dish, mix panko, sage, thyme, savory, pepper and the remaining salt. Drain chicken, discarding marinade. Dip chicken pieces, one at a time, into egg mixture; coat with crumb mixture.

4. Arrange chicken in prepared baking pan so pieces are not touching. Sprinkle with any remaining crumb mixture.

5. Bake, uncovered, in a 375° oven about 30 minutes or until chicken is no longer pink (170°). Do not turn pieces while baking. **Makes 4 servings.**

Curried Oven-Fried Chicken: Prepare as above, except substitute 1½ teaspoons curry powder for the sage, thyme and savory.

Per serving: 262 cal, 4 g fat, 137 mg chol, 453 mg sodium, 15 g carbo, 1 g fiber, 38 g pro.

After the gray days of winter fade away, the eye-catching colors of spring flowers refresh the landscape and the spirit.

Cranberry-Stuffed Chicken Burgers

PREP 25 minutes **GRILL** 17 minutes

¼ cup orange juice
⅓ cup dried cranberries
1½ pounds uncooked ground chicken
⅓ cup fine dry bread crumbs
1 tablespoon snipped fresh marjoram or
   1 teaspoon dried marjoram, crushed
¼ teaspoon kosher salt or ⅛ teaspoon salt
1 to 2 ounces Parmesan cheese, shaved
4 thin slices fresh mozzarella cheese or
   4 slices regular mozzarella cheese
4 kaiser rolls or sesame hamburger buns,
   split and toasted
  Lettuce leaves

1. In a small saucepan, bring orange juice to boiling. Remove from heat; stir in cranberries. Let stand for 5 minutes. Drain cranberries, discarding orange juice.

2. Meanwhile, in a large bowl, combine ground chicken, bread crumbs, marjoram and salt. Shape chicken mixture into eight ½-inch-thick patties. (The mixture may be sticky. If necessary, wet hands when shaping patties.)

3. Place one-fourth of the cranberries and one-fourth of the Parmesan cheese on the center of each of four patties. Top with the remaining patties; press edges to seal.

4. For a charcoal grill: Grill patties on the greased rack of an uncovered grill directly over medium coals for 14 to 18 minutes or until no longer pink (165°)*, turning once halfway through grilling. (For a gas grill: Preheat grill. Reduce heat to medium.

Place patties on greased grill rack over heat. Cover; grill as above.) Top each burger with a slice of mozzarella cheese. Grill, uncovered, about 3 minutes more or until cheese begins to melt. Serve burgers on toasted rolls with lettuce leaves. **Makes 4 servings.**

*Note: The internal color of a burger is not a reliable doneness indicator. A chicken patty cooked to 165° is safe, regardless of color. To measure the doneness of a patty, insert an instant-read thermometer through the side of the patty to a depth of 2 to 3 inches.

Per serving: 552 cal, 22 g fat, 161 mg chol, 762 mg sodium, 47 g carbo, 3 g fiber, 42 g pro.

A chicken burger just may be the perfect first burger of the grilling season. In contrast to its beefier cousins, this fruit-and-cheese-stuffed poultry patty is fresh and light—just like the air in spring.

Chicken Enchiladas Adobo

Using just one chipotle chile pepper from the can means you will have leftover chiles and sauce. Divide the leftovers into one- to two-chile portions in small sealable containers or plastic bags and freeze for future use.

PREP 20 minutes **COOK** 15 minutes **COOL** 5 minutes **BAKE** 25 minutes

1 14.5-ounce can diced fire-roasted tomatoes, undrained
¾ cup water
1 medium onion, chopped
1 chipotle chile pepper in adobo sauce
1 tablespoon adobo sauce (optional)
1 tablespoon snipped fresh cilantro
1 teaspoon ground cumin
½ teaspoon chili powder
½ teaspoon kosher salt or ¼ teaspoon salt
1 tablespoon vegetable oil
1 pound skinless, boneless chicken breast halves or skinless, boneless chicken thighs, cut into bite-size strips
½ cup corn and black bean salsa
½ cup sour cream
½ teaspoon finely shredded lime peel
8 multigrain or whole wheat flour tortillas
¾ cup shredded Chihuahua cheese or Monterey Jack cheese (3 ounces)
1 2¼-ounce can sliced pitted ripe olives, drained
½ cup sliced green onions (4)

1. Lightly grease a 13x9x2-inch baking dish; set aside.

2. For sauce, in a medium saucepan, mix undrained tomatoes, the water, chopped onion, chipotle pepper, adobo sauce (if you like), cilantro, cumin, chili powder and half of the salt. Bring to boiling; reduce heat. Simmer, uncovered, for 15 minutes. Remove from heat; let cool for 5 minutes. Place in a blender or food processor. Cover and blend or process until smooth.

3. Meanwhile, in a large skillet, cook chicken in hot oil over medium heat until browned and no longer pink. Remove from heat; drain off fat. Stir in salsa, sour cream, lime peel and the remaining salt.

4. To assemble enchiladas, spoon ½ cup sauce into bottom of prepared baking dish. Spoon about 3 tablespoons of the chicken mixture onto each tortilla near edge; roll up. Place tortillas, seam sides down, in prepared baking dish. Pour remaining sauce over all.

5. Bake, covered, in a 375° oven for 15 minutes. Uncover and sprinkle with cheese. Bake 10 to 15 minutes more or until heated through. Sprinkle with olives and green onions. **Makes 8 servings.**

Per serving: 259 cal, 10 g fat, 50 mg chol, 702 mg sodium, 22 g carbo, 5 g fiber, 19 g pro.

On a cool spring night, a casserole bubbling from the oven will still get a warm welcome from hungry guests at your table.

Turkey with Creamy Morel Sauce

If you can't find fresh morels, rehydrate dried ones by covering them with warm water for 30 to 45 minutes. Drain and measure ¾ cup.

START TO FINISH 30 minutes

3 tablespoons all-purpose flour
¼ teaspoon salt
¼ teaspoon lemon-pepper seasoning
4 turkey breast steaks or 4 medium skinless, boneless chicken breast halves (12 ounces total)
3 tablespoons butter
2 ounces fresh morels or ½ ounce dried morels, rehydrated
2 tablespoons sliced green onion
1 clove garlic, minced
1¼ cups half-and-half, light cream or milk
1 tablespoon all-purpose flour
1 tablespoon dry sherry
Salt and ground black pepper
Fresh herbs (optional)

1. Combine the 3 tablespoons flour, the salt and lemon-pepper seasoning; coat turkey with flour mixture.

2. In a large skillet, cook turkey in 2 tablespoons of the butter over medium heat for 8 to 10 minutes or until tender and no pink remains, turning once. Transfer turkey to individual plates; cover to keep warm.

3. Cut any large morels into bite-size strips. For sauce: In the same skillet cook morels, green onion and garlic in the remaining butter for 3 to 4 minutes or until tender.

4. Combine half-and-half and the 1 tablespoon flour; add to vegetables in skillet. Cook and stir until thickened and bubbly; add sherry. Cook and stir for 1 minute more. Season to taste with salt and pepper.

5. Spoon some of the sauce over turkey; pass remainder when serving. If you like, garnish with fresh herbs. **Makes 4 servings.**

Per serving: 301 cal, 18 g fat, 83 mg chol, 324 mg sodium, 11 g carbo, 23 g pro.

In the dull seam between winter and spring, a delightfully rich delicacy emerges—oh-so-briefly—and excites the Midwest palate. Welcome, elusive morel mushroom.

SMOKED
TROUT CAKES

Smoked Trout Cakes

PREP 25 minutes **COOK** 4 minutes per batch

  4 green onions, thinly sliced
  ¼ cup finely chopped green sweet pepper
  ¼ cup finely chopped red sweet pepper
  ¼ cup mayonnaise
  ¼ cup Dijon-style or Creole mustard
  1 clove garlic, minced
  2 tablespoons lemon juice
  1 to 2 tablespoons capers, drained
  1 teaspoon Old Bay Seasoning
  ⅛ teaspoon cayenne pepper
  1 pound smoked trout, whitefish or salmon, flaked, with skin and bones removed (3½ cups)
  1 cup panko (Japanese-style bread crumbs) or soft French bread crumbs
  2 tablespoons olive oil or vegetable oil
     Lemon wedges (optional)

1. In a large bowl, combine onions, green and red sweet pepper, mayonnaise, mustard, garlic, lemon juice, drained capers, seasoning and cayenne pepper. Add fish and bread crumbs. Mix well. Shape trout mixture into twelve 2½- to 3-inch-diameter patties.

2. In a large skillet, cook trout cakes, half at a time, in hot oil for 4 to 5 minutes or until lightly browned and heated through, turning once halfway through cooking. Transfer trout cakes to an ovenproof serving platter or cookie sheet. Keep warm in a 300° oven while cooking remaining patties. (If necessary, add more oil during cooking.)

3. If you like, serve trout cakes with lemon wedges. **Makes 12 cakes.**

Per cake: 142 cal, 8 g fat, 45 mg chol, 373 mg sodium, 9 g carbo, 0 g fiber, 7 g pro.

Golden Trout

PREP 25 minutes **COOK** 6 minutes

  1 tablespoon olive oil
  2 8-ounce fresh golden trout or other trout fillets or whitefish fillets
  2 tablespoons all-purpose flour
     Salt and pepper
  8 ounces morel or other mushrooms (such as crimini, shiitake and/or button), halved
  2 cloves garlic, minced
  1 tablespoon butter
  1 7½-ounce can tomatoes, cut up, or half of a 14½-ounce can diced tomatoes with basil, oregano and garlic
  ½ cup dry white wine or chicken broth
  12 fresh asparagus spears (about 8 ounces), cooked until crisp-tender*

1. Rinse trout; pat dry with paper towels. In a plastic bag, combine 1 tablespoon of the flour, ¼ teaspoon salt and ⅛ teaspoon pepper. Add fish to bag and shake to coat.

2. In large skillet, cook fillets skin sides down in hot oil, for 3 minutes; turn and cook for 3 minutes more or until fish flakes easily with a fork. Transfer to a platter; keep warm.

3. In a plastic bag, place remaining flour, ⅛ teaspoon salt and dash pepper. Add mushrooms and shake to coat. In same skillet, cook mushrooms and garlic in hot butter for 3 minutes or until browned.

4. Add tomatoes and wine; cook and stir until bubbly, loosening browned bits. Reduce heat and boil gently, uncovered, for 5 to 6 minutes or until sauce is slightly thickened. Add asparagus; heat through. Serve sauce over fish. **Makes 2 servings.**

*Note: Cook asparagus in a small amount of boiling water for 4 to 6 minutes or until crisp-tender.

Per serving: 592 cal, 27 g fat, 149 mg chol, 671 mg sodium, 23 g carbo, 7 g fiber, 53 g pro.

Salmon-Asparagus Pasta

PREP 30 minutes **GRILL** 4 minutes

  8 ounces dried penne or other pasta
  12 ounces asparagus spears, trimmed and cut into bite-size pieces (save a few whole spears for garnish)
  ½ cup chicken broth
  ¼ cup finely chopped red sweet pepper
  1 clove garlic, minced
  ½ teaspoon dried basil, crushed, or
     ¼ teaspoon dried dillweed
  ⅛ teaspoon salt
  ¼ cup lemon juice
  ¼ cup olive oil
  4 4-ounce fresh tuna or salmon steaks, cut ½ inch thick

1. Cook pasta according to package directions, adding asparagus pieces and spears for the last 5 minutes of cooking. Drain; set aside any whole spears.

2. Meanwhile, in a small saucepan, combine the chicken broth, sweet pepper, garlic, basil and salt. Bring to boiling. Reduce heat. Boil gently, uncovered, for 10 to 12 minutes or until most of the liquid evaporates. Stir in lemon juice and oil; set aside.

3. Rinse fish; pat dry. Place the fish steaks on the greased rack of an uncovered grill directly over medium-hot coals. Grill for 4 to 6 minutes or until fish flakes easily with a fork. (Or broil or poach fish until done.)

4. Toss hot pasta mixture with broth mixture. Serve the fish over the pasta. Garnish with asparagus spears. **Makes 4 servings.**

Per serving: 484 cal, 16 g fat, 51 mg chol, 251 mg sodium, 48 g carbo, 3 g fiber, 36 g pro.

Dutch Lettuce

A warm bacon dressing tops lettuce and potatoes in this side-dish salad.

START TO FINISH 30 minutes

    6 slices bacon, chopped
    ¼ cup vinegar
    2 teaspoons sugar
    5 to 6 cups torn Boston or buttercrunch
       lettuce
    3 small cooked potatoes, peeled and sliced
    2 hard-cooked eggs, peeled and chopped
    2 tablespoons chopped onion

1. In a large skillet, cook bacon until crisp. With a slotted spoon, transfer bacon pieces to paper towels to drain; set aside. Reserve drippings.

2. Stir vinegar and sugar into bacon drippings in skillet. Bring to boiling. Remove from heat and keep warm.

3. In a salad bowl, gently mix together the lettuce, potatoes, eggs and onion. Pour warm dressing over. Toss. Sprinkle with bacon; toss again. **Makes 6 servings.**

Per serving: 217 cal, 17 g fat, 79 mg chol, 170 mg sodium, 10 g carbo, 1 g fiber, 6 g pro.

Fingerling Potato Salad with Honey-Thyme Vinaigrette

You will have more vinaigrette than you need, but that's ok. It will keep for a few weeks in the refrigerator and makes a great vinaigrette for another potato salad or pasta salad, or even on a regular tossed green salad.

PREP 30 minutes **COOK** 9 minutes **STAND** 5 minutes **CHILL** 2 to 24 hours

    1½ pounds white or yellow fingerling
         potatoes
     1 teaspoon kosher salt
     8 ounces fresh haricots verts or tender
         young green beans
     3 cups water
    ¼ cup cider vinegar
     1 medium shallot, halved
     2 tablespoons honey
     1 tablespoon fresh thyme leaves
    1½ teaspoons Dijon-style mustard
    ⅛ teaspoon kosher salt
    ⅛ teaspoon ground black pepper
    ½ cup canola or vegetable oil
     1 small red onion, halved and thinly sliced
     1 pound bacon, crisp-cooked, drained and
         crumbled
    ½ cup crumbled feta cheese (2 ounces)

1. Scrub the potatoes. In a large saucepan, cook potatoes and the 1 teaspoon kosher salt, covered, in enough boiling water to cover for 8 to 10 minutes or just until tender; drain well. Spread out in a single layer in a shallow baking pan to cool. When cool enough to handle, halve potatoes lengthwise. Set aside.

2. Wash haricots verts; trim and (if you like) halve crosswise. In a medium saucepan, bring the 3 cups water to boiling. Add haricots verts. Return to boiling. Simmer, uncovered, for 1 to 2 minutes or just until crisp-tender. Drain; plunge into a large bowl half-filled with ice water. Let stand 5 minutes; drain well. Set aside.

3. For vinaigrette: In a food processor or blender, combine vinegar, shallot, honey, thyme, mustard, ⅛ teaspoon kosher salt and the pepper. Cover and process or blend until combined. With processor or blender running, slowly add oil in a steady stream until vinaigrette is thickened.

4. In a large salad bowl, combine potatoes, haricots verts and red onion. Drizzle with enough of the vinaigrette to thoroughly coat. Cover and chill for 2 to 24 hours.

5. Just before serving, toss salad with bacon and top with feta cheese. Serve with remaining vinaigrette or reserve vinaigrette for another use. **Makes 8 to 10 servings.**

Per serving: 324 cal, 22 g fat, 24 mg chol, 753 mg sodium, 23 g carbo, 3 g fiber, 9 g pro.

FINGERLING POTATO SALAD WITH HONEY-THYME VINAIGRETTE

Crunchy Asian Noodle Slaw

PREP 30 minutes **BAKE** 10 minutes
CHILL up to 2 hours

1 tablespoon white sesame seeds
1 tablespoon black or white sesame seeds
1 teaspoon celery seeds
⅓ cup sesame oil (not toasted), peanut oil or vegetable oil
⅓ cup rice vinegar or cider vinegar
2 tablespoons sugar
1 teaspoon grated fresh ginger or 1 tablespoon finely chopped pickled ginger
1 tablespoon reduced-sodium soy sauce
⅛ to ¼ teaspoon crushed red pepper
1 3-ounce package chicken- or beef-flavored ramen noodles, broken into small pieces
4 cups shredded green cabbage (about ½ of a medium head) or half of a 16-ounce package shredded cabbage with carrot (coleslaw mix)
2 cups fresh broccoli florets, coarsely chopped

1. In a shallow baking pan, spread out sesame seeds and celery seeds. Bake in a 300° oven about 10 minutes or until lightly toasted, stirring once. Remove from oven; cool.

2. For dressing: In a screw-top jar, combine oil, vinegar, sugar, ginger, soy sauce, red pepper, seasonings from the flavoring packet of ramen noodles and toasted seeds. Cover and shake well; set aside.

3. In a large bowl, toss together the broken dry ramen noodles, cabbage and broccoli. Shake the dressing well; pour over the cabbage mixture. Toss lightly to coat. Serve immediately for maximum crispness or cover and chill for up to 2 hours before serving. **Makes 8 to 10 side-dish servings.**

Per serving: 176 cal, 12 g fat, 0 mg chol, 282 mg sodium, 14 g carbo, 2 g fiber, 3 g pro.

Nutty Apple-Cherry Slaw

PREP 30 minutes **CHILL** up to 24 hours

⅓ cup sunflower oil, vegetable oil or olive oil
3 tablespoons cider vinegar or white wine vinegar
3 tablespoons orange juice
1 tablespoon honey or sugar
1½ teaspoons Dijon-style mustard or coarse-ground mustard
¼ teaspoon salt
Dash ground cinnamon or ground nutmeg (optional)
4 cups shredded* red cabbage (about ½ of a medium head) or half of a 16-ounce package shredded cabbage with carrot (coleslaw mix)
2 cups loosely packed fresh arugula and/or watercress (thick stems discarded), rinsed and dried, or desired greens (such as fresh baby spinach, mesclun or torn mixed salad greens)
1 medium Granny Smith or Golden Delicious apple, cored and sliced into thin strips or coarsely chopped
½ cup dried cherries, dried cranberries, currants or raisins
2 tablespoons thinly sliced green onion
¼ cup dry-roasted sunflower kernels or ⅓ cup chopped pecans, hickory nuts or walnuts

1. For vinaigrette: In a screw-top jar, combine oil, vinegar, orange juice, honey, mustard, salt and, if you like, cinnamon. Cover and shake well; set aside.

2. In a large bowl, toss together cabbage, arugula apple, cherries and green onion. Shake the vinaigrette well; pour over the cabbage mixture. Toss lightly to coat. Sprinkle with sunflower kernels. Serve immediately for maximum crispness or cover and chill for up to 24 hours before serving. **Makes 8 to 10 side-dish servings.**

***Note:** To shred cabbage, using a large chef's knife, cut cabbage head into wedges and remove core. Thinly slice the cored cabbage wedge across the grain of the leaves.

Per serving: 165 cal, 11 g fat, 0 mg chol, 125 mg sodium, 17 g carbo, 2 g fiber, 2 g pro.

Delicate greens—arugula, frisée and dandelion among them—are some of the first things to appear at Midwest farmers markets.

Sugar Snap Peas with Sesame Seeds

START TO FINISH 20 minutes

    3 cups fresh sugar snap peas (about
       12 ounces) or frozen loose-pack sugar
       snap peas
    1 teaspoon grated fresh ginger
    2 teaspoons butter
 1½ teaspoons toasted sesame oil
    ½ teaspoon salt
    ⅛ teaspoon freshly ground black pepper
    1 teaspoon white sesame seeds, toasted*
    1 teaspoon black sesame seeds

1. Remove strings and tips from fresh peas. Cook fresh peas, covered, in a small amount of boiling salted water for 3 to 5 minutes or until crisp-tender. (Or cook frozen peas according to package directions.) Drain well. Transfer peas to a large bowl; set aside.

2. In a small saucepan, cook ginger in hot butter for 1 minute. Remove from heat. Stir in toasted sesame oil, salt and pepper. Pour butter mixture over hot cooked peas; toss to coat. Sprinkle with sesame seeds. Serve warm, at room temperature or chilled. **Makes 4 side-dish servings.**

*Note: Sesame seeds have a mildly sweet, nutty flavor that is enhanced by toasting. To toast, spread sesame seeds in a thin layer in a shallow, ungreased pan. A pie plate works well. Toast in a 350° oven about 10 minutes, stirring once or twice. It is best to store sesame seeds in the refrigerator or freezer because they have a high amount of oil so tend to go rancid.

Per serving: 85 cal, 4 g fat, 5 mg chol, 304 mg sodium, 8 g carbo, 2 g fiber, 3 g pro.

Oven-Roasted Asparagus with Lemon-Chive Butter

PREP 15 minutes **ROAST** 8 minutes
STAND 30 minutes **CHILL** 1 hour

       Lemon Chive Butter (recipe follows)
 1½ pounds asparagus spears
    1 to 2 tablespoons olive oil
    1 to 2 cloves garlic, minced

1. Prepare the Lemon Chive Butter.

2. Snap off woody base of one spear. Trim remaining spears even with the first. Wash the asparagus. Drain well on paper towels. If you like, use a vegetable peeler to scrape off the scales from the asparagus.

3. Place asparagus in a large resealable plastic storage bag. Add oil and garlic. Seal the bag. Lay the bag down on the counter and working from the outside of the bag roll the asparagus with your fingers to massage the seasonings onto the spears.

4. Place the asparagus spears on a shallow pan lined with foil. Drizzle oil in the bag over the spears. Bake, uncovered, in a 425° oven for 8 to 10 minutes or until the asparagus is crisp-tender. (Avoid overcooking. Asparagus retains its rich, bright green color when roasted in the oven.)

5. To serve, transfer to a serving platter. Cut the Lemon Chive Butter into ½-inch-thick slices. Place desired number of slices of butter on top of asparagus. (Roll up and refrigerate or freeze remaining butter for another use. The butter can be used on baked or grilled fish or chicken or vegetables.) **Makes 6 to 8 side-dish servings.**

Lemon Chive Butter: Allow ½ cup butter (no substitute) to stand at room temperature for 30 minutes. In small a bowl or on a large plate, stir together softened butter; 2 tablespoons finely snipped fresh chives; 2 teaspoons finely shredded lemon peel; 1 clove garlic, minced; and ⅛ teaspoon salt until well combined. Transfer to a sheet of waxed paper. Shape into a 4-inch-long roll. Wrap in waxed paper; twist ends to seal. Chill in the refrigerator for at least 1 hour or until firm. Makes about ½ cup.

Per serving: 105 cal, 10 g fat, 22 mg chol, 83 mg sodium, 3 g carbo, 1 g fiber, 1 g pro.

Crispened New Potatoes

PREP 25 minutes **BAKE** 20 minutes

1¼ pounds tiny new potatoes (about 24)
2 tablespoons yellow cornmeal
2 tablespoons all-purpose flour
1 tablespoon oat bran
2 tablespoons grated Parmesan cheese
1 tablespoon finely snipped fresh parsley
½ teaspoon snipped fresh dill or
    ¼ teaspoon dried dillweed
½ teaspoon paprika
1 egg white
¼ cup fat-free milk
    Nonstick cooking spray or cooking oil
3 tablespoons butter or margarine, melted

1. Cook whole potatoes in lightly salted boiling water for 15 minutes. Drain; rinse in cold water. Drain. Halve or quarter large potatoes.

2. In a shallow dish, combine cornmeal, flour and oat bran. Add Parmesan cheese, parsley, dill and paprika.

3. In another shallow dish, whisk together egg white and milk. Lightly coat a 12x7x2-inch baking dish with nonstick cooking spray.

4. Dip potatoes in egg white mixture; dip into flour mixture. Place in prepared baking dish; drizzle with butter.

5. Bake, covered, in a 400° oven for 10 minutes. Uncover; bake for 10 minutes more or until potatoes are tender. **Makes 4 to 5 side-dish servings.**

Per serving: 231 cal, 10 g fat, 25 mg chol, 161 mg sodium, 31 g carbo, 3 g fiber, 6 g pro.

Morel and Potato au Gratin

PREP 25 minutes **BAKE** 55 minutes

6 ounces fresh morel mushrooms* or other
    fresh mushrooms
1 tablespoon butter
3 leeks, sliced ½ inch thick
2 tablespoons butter
2 tablespoons all-purpose flour
2 teaspoons snipped fresh oregano
¼ teaspoon freshly ground black pepper
⅛ teaspoon salt
2 cups milk
2 pounds Yukon gold potatoes or other
    potatoes (such as long white, round
    white or round red, peeled and sliced
    ¼ inch thick)
1 cup shredded Jarlsberg cheese or white
    cheddar cheese (4 ounces)
½ cup seasoned dry bread crumbs
¼ cup finely shredded Parmesan cheese
3 tablespoons butter, melted

1. Clean morel mushrooms by rinsing them for several minutes in a pitcher tilted under a running faucet so that it spills over. Pat dry with paper towels. Wash other mushrooms by gently wiping with a damp towel or paper towel. Trim stem ends. Slice mushrooms (should measure 2¼ cups). Set aside.

2. In a medium skillet, cook leeks in the 1 tablespoon butter over medium heat, stirring frequently, for 5 minutes. Stir in mushrooms. Cook and stir for 5 minutes more; remove from heat and set aside. In a medium saucepan, melt the 2 tablespoons butter over medium heat. Stir in the flour, oregano, pepper and salt. Add milk all at once. Cook and stir over medium heat until thickened and bubbly. Gently stir in mushroom mixture.

3. Arrange half of the sliced potatoes to cover the bottom of a lightly greased 3-quart rectangular baking dish, overlapping as necessary. Sprinkle with half of the cheese. Pour half of the sauce over potatoes. Repeat with the remaining potatoes, cheese and sauce.

4. In a small bowl, stir together the bread crumbs, Parmesan cheese and the 3 tablespoons melted butter. Sprinkle over the potatoes.

5. Bake, covered, in a 350° oven for 40 minutes. Uncover and bake about 15 minutes more or until potatoes are tender when pierced with a knife. **Makes 8 side-dish servings.**

*Note: If fresh morels aren't available, substitute 2 ounces dried morel or porcini mushrooms. In a small bowl, cover the dried mushrooms with hot water. Let stand for 20 minutes. Rinse under warm running water; squeeze out excess moisture. Slice the mushrooms.

Per serving: 313 cal, 16 g fat, 45 mg chol, 429 mg sodium, 33 g carbo, 2 g fiber, 12 g pro.

In spring, the landscape is truly in the pink. Flowering trees line the walking paths in Cincinnati's Eden Park, which is home to the Cincinnati Art Museum, Cincinnati Playhouse in the Park and the Krohn Conservatory. Landmarks within the park include the Hinkle Magnolia Garden.

Indiana Sugar Cream Pie

PREP 25 minutes **BAKE** 55 minutes

Pastry for a Single-Crust Pie* (see recipe, page 102)
1 cup packed brown sugar
⅓ cup all-purpose flour
2 cups (1 pint) half-and-half or light cream
1 teaspoon vanilla
2 tablespoons butter, cut into small pieces
Ground nutmeg

1. Prepare Pastry for a Single-Crust Pie. On a lightly floured surface, use your hands to slightly flatten dough. Roll dough from center to edges into a 12-inch circle. Wrap pastry circle around rolling pin; unroll into a 9-inch pie plate. Ease pastry into pie plate without stretching it. Trim pastry to ½ inch beyond edge of pie plate. Fold under extra pastry even with edge of plate. Crimp edge as desired. Do not prick pastry.

2. In a small bowl, combine brown sugar and flour. In another small bowl, combine half-and-half and vanilla. Evenly spread brown sugar mixture in the bottom of the pastry-lined pie plate. Pour half-and-half mixture over brown sugar mixture. Evenly distribute butter pieces over top of pie. Lightly sprinkle with nutmeg.

3. To prevent overbrowning, cover edge of pie with foil. Bake in a 350° oven for 25 minutes. Remove foil. Bake about 30 minutes more or until top is lightly browned and pie is bubbly all over. (Pie will not appear set.) Cool on a wire rack. Cover and chill in refrigerator. **Makes 10 servings.**

*Note: To save time, use half of a 15-ounce package (one crust) rolled refrigerated unbaked piecrust instead of the homemade pastry. Let stand according to package directions before easing into pie plate.

Per serving: 336 cal, 17 g fat, 36 mg chol, 192 mg sodium, 41 g carbo, 1 g fiber, 4 g pro.

Some say empty apple bins inspired Hoosier Quakers to create this single-crust dessert of sugar, cream and flour. The ingredients list may make you think something's missing. But try it and you'll see why the humble phenomenon became Indiana's official pie in 2009.

Rhubarb Custard Pie

The much-anticipated, though fleeting, time in spring when juicy rhubarb is at its peak is the perfect time to make a pie.

PREP 50 minutes **BAKE** 45 minutes

Pastry for Double-Crust Pie (recipe
   follows)
1½ to 2 cups sugar
¼ cup all-purpose flour
½ teaspoon ground cinnamon
   Dash salt
4 cups fresh or frozen unsweetened
   chopped rhubarb
2 slightly beaten eggs
2 tablespoons half-and-half or light cream
   or milk
   Milk and sugar (optional)

1. On a lightly floured surface, roll out half of the pastry and fit into a 9-inch pie plate. Trim to ½ inch beyond edge of pie plate for lattice top, or trim even with rim for a two-crust pie.

2. In mixing bowl, combine 1½ cups sugar, flour, cinnamon and salt. Add the rhubarb. Gently toss until coated. (For frozen fruit, let stand for 15 to 30 minutes or until partially thawed but icy.)

3. In a small bowl, whisk together eggs and cream. Pour over fruit; toss to mix. Transfer to the pasty-lined pie plate.

4. On a lightly floured surface, roll out remaining dough into a 12-inch circle and cut slits for steam to escape or cut into ½-inch-wide strips for lattice top. Place pastry over filling and weave strips over top for lattice. Press ends of strips into crust rim and fold bottom pastry over strips. For a two-crust pie, trim top crust to ½ inch beyond edge of pie plate; fold extra pastry under bottom pastry and flute edge. If you like, make leaf cutouts from pastry scraps and place on pie; brush top crust with milk and sprinkle with additional sugar.

5. To prevent overbrowning, cover edge of pie with foil. Bake in a 375° oven for 25 minutes for fresh fruit (50 minutes for frozen). Remove foil. Bake for 20 to 25 minutes more or until top is golden. Cool on wire rack. **Makes 8 servings.**

Per serving: 457 cal, 18 g fat, 48 mg chol, 187 mg sodium, 68 g carbo, 2 g fiber, 6 g pro.

Pastry for Double-Crust Pie: In a large bowl, stir together 2 cups all-purpose flour and ½ teaspoon salt. Using a pastry blender, cut in ⅔ cup shortening until pieces are pea-size. Sprinkle 1 tablespoon of cold water over part of the mixture; gently toss with a fork. Push moistened dough to the side of the bowl. Repeat moistening dough, using 1 tablespoon cold water at a time, until all the dough is moistened (6 to 7 tablespoons cold water total). Divide dough in half. Form each half into a ball. Proceed as directed in recipe method.

Rhubarb-Lemon Chiffon Pie

A colorful rhubarb sauce and a tangy lemon filling team up for first-rate results in this refreshing pie.

PREP 1 hour **CHILL** 8 hours

1 3-ounce package lemon-flavored
   gelatin mix
1 cup boiling water
½ cup sugar
2 teaspoons finely shredded lemon peel
3 tablespoons lemon juice
1 cup whipping cream
2 cups Rosy Rhubarb Sauce (recipe follows)
   Baked Pastry Shell (see recipe, page 106)

1. Dissolve gelatin in the boiling water. Stir in sugar until dissolved. Add lemon peel and juice; stir until combined. Cover; chill until lemon mixture is the consistency of unbeaten egg whites.

2. In a medium bowl, beat cream until soft peaks form (tips curl). Fold whipped cream and Rosy Rhubarb Sauce into lemon mixture. Chill until mixture mounds. Pile into Baked Pastry Shell. Cover and chill in the refrigerator for 8 hours or until firm. **Makes 10 to 12 servings.**

Per serving: 374 cal, 16 g fat, 33 mg chol, 103 mg sodium, 57 g carbo, 2 g fiber, 3 g pro.

Rosy Rhubarb Sauce: In a saucepan, mix 1¼ to 1½ cups sugar, 1 tablespoon water and 1 tablespoon finely shredded orange peel. Bring to boiling. Add 6 cups fresh or frozen rhubarb, sliced ½ inch thick. Simmer, uncovered, about 8 minutes or until rhubarb is tender and mixture is thickened, stirring as necessary to prevent sticking. Cool. Chill in the refrigerator.

RHUBARB-LEMON
CHIFFON PIE

Missouri Gooey Butter Cake

A baker's honest mix-up (swapping the amounts of flour and sugar) led to the happy mistake of this beloved St. Louis dessert. It's always true to its sticky name, but now bakeries offer it in flavors such as chocolate, peanut butter and apple.

PREP 20 minutes **BAKE** 35 minutes

  1 cup all-purpose flour
  3 tablespoons granulated sugar
  ⅓ cup butter
1¼ cups granulated sugar
  ¾ cup butter, softened
  ¼ cup light-color corn syrup
  1 egg
  1 cup all-purpose flour
  1 5-ounce can evaporated milk
     Powdered sugar (optional)

1. For crust: In a medium bowl, combine 1 cup flour and the 3 tablespoons granulated sugar. Using a pastry blender, cut in the ⅓ cup butter until mixture resembles fine crumbs. Pat crust into the bottom of an ungreased 9x9x2-inch baking pan.

2. For filling: In a large mixing bowl, beat the 1¼ cups granulated sugar and the ¾ cup butter with an electric mixer on medium speed until combined. Beat in corn syrup and egg just until combined.

3. Alternately add the 1 cup flour and the evaporated milk to beaten butter mixture, beating on low speed after each addition just until combined (batter will appear slightly curdled). Pour over crust in pan. Spread batter evenly to edges of pan.

4. Bake in a 350° oven about 35 minutes or until cake is nearly firm when gently shaken. Cool in pan on a wire rack. If you like, sprinkle with powdered sugar before serving. **Makes 12 servings.**

Per serving: 358 cal, 18 g fat, 65 mg chol, 143 mg sodium, 46 g carbo, 1 g fiber, 4 g pro.

The sun peeks over a horizon awash in wildflowers. Midwesterners hike, bike and bird-watch through their beloved tallgrass prairies.

Maple Syrup Cake

PREP 30 minutes **BAKE** 45 minutes **COOL** 10 minutes

2½ cups cake flour or 2¼ cups all-purpose
     flour
 2 teaspoons baking powder
½ teaspoon baking soda
½ teaspoon salt
½ teaspoon ground ginger
½ cup butter, softened
½ cup sugar
 1 egg, lightly beaten
 1 egg yolk, lightly beaten
 1 cup pure maple syrup
½ cup hot water
     Maple Syrup Icing (recipe follows)
½ cup coarsely chopped walnuts, toasted
     (optional)

1. Grease and flour a 10-inch fluted tube pan; set pan aside. In a medium bowl, combine flour, baking powder, baking soda, salt and ginger; set aside.

2. In a large mixing bowl, beat butter with an electric mixer on medium to high speed for 30 seconds. Add sugar; beat until well combined. Add egg, egg yolk and maple syrup; beat for 1 minute more. Alternately add flour mixture and the hot water to butter mixture, beating on low speed after each addition until combined. Spoon batter into the prepared pan; spread evenly.

3. Bake in a 375° oven for 45 minutes or until a wooden toothpick inserted near the center comes out clean. Cool cake in pan on a wire rack for 10 minutes. Remove cake from pan. Cool completely. Spoon Maple Syrup Icing over cake and, if you like, sprinkle top with walnuts. **Makes 12 servings.**

Maple Syrup Icing: In a medium mixing bowl, beat ½ cup powdered sugar and 2 tablespoons softened butter with an electric mixer on medium speed until combined. Beat in ¼ cup pure maple syrup. Beat in 1 cup additional powdered sugar. Add milk, 1 teaspoon at a time, to make drizzling consistency. Makes about 1 cup.

Per serving: 409 cal, 14 g fat, 61 mg chol, 268 mg sodium, 69 g carbo, 1 g fiber, 4 g pro.

At the first blush of spring, sap from maple trees in the covered-bridge country of Parke County, Indiana, is collected and turned into sweet liquid gold.

Rhubarb Cheesecake

PREP 45 minutes **COOK** 5 minutes **BAKE** 1 hour 30 minutes **COOL** 45 minutes **CHILL** 4 hours

2½ cups thinly sliced fresh or frozen rhubarb, thawed
⅓ cup sugar
2 tablespoons orange juice
8 1-ounce squares white baking chocolate with cocoa butter
2 cups finely crushed graham crackers (about 20 squares)
⅓ cup butter, melted
3 8-ounce packages cream cheese, softened
1 16-ounce carton dairy sour cream
½ cup sugar
1 tablespoon cornstarch
2 teaspoons vanilla
½ teaspoon salt
3 eggs
Whipped cream (optional)
White baking chocolate curls (optional)
Mint leaves (optional)

1. In a medium saucepan, combine rhubarb, the ⅓ cup sugar and the orange juice. Bring just to boiling; reduce heat. Cook, uncovered, about 5 minutes or until rhubarb is tender, stirring occasionally; set aside.

2. In a small heavy saucepan, melt white chocolate baking squares over very low heat, stirring occasionally. Set aside to cool.

3. In a medium bowl, combine graham crackers and butter. Press crumb mixture onto the bottom and about 1½ inches up the sides of a 10-inch springform pan. Wrap outside of the springform pan securely with heavy foil. Set aside.

4. In a very large bowl, beat cream cheese, sour cream, the ½ cup sugar, cornstarch, vanilla and salt with electric mixer on medium speed until well blended. Add eggs, one at a time, beating just until combined after each addition. Gradually beat in melted white chocolate until combined.

5. Pour half of the filling into crust-lined pan. Spoon 1 cup of the rhubarb sauce over the filling, spreading evenly. Top with remaining filling. Spoon remaining rhubarb sauce over filling. Using the back of a spoon, gently swirl the rhubarb mixture into the filling.

6. Place springform pan in a large roasting pan. (Make sure there is at least 1 inch between springform pan and edges of roasting pan.) Place roasting pan on oven rack. Carefully pour enough boiling water into roasting pan to come halfway up sides of springform pan.

7. Bake in a 350° oven for 1½ to 2 hours or until edge of cheesecake is firm and center appears nearly set when lightly shaken. Check water level every 30 minutes, adding more water if needed. Carefully remove cheesecake pan from water bath; transfer to a wire rack and cool for 15 minutes. Remove foil. Loosen cheesecake from sides of pan by carefully running a knife around the edge of the pan. Cool cheesecake for 30 minutes more. Remove sides of pan and cool completely. Cover cheesecake with plastic wrap and chill at least 4 hours before serving.

8. If you like, just before serving, pipe rosettes of whipped cream on the top of the cheesecake and garnish with white baking bar curls and mint. Cut into wedges. **Makes 12 to 14 servings.**

Make-ahead tip: Prepare, bake and thoroughly cool the cheesecake. Cover tightly with plastic wrap. Store in the refrigerator for up to 2 days.

Per serving: 586 cal, 42 g fat, 149 mg chol, 493 mg sodium, 42 g carbo, 1 g fiber, 10 g pro.

Honey-Rosemary Shortbread Cookies

PREP 35 minutes **BAKE** 15 minutes per batch

 2 cups all-purpose flour
 ⅔ cup sugar
 2 to 3 teaspoons snipped fresh rosemary
 1 teaspoon kosher salt
 ¾ cup cold unsalted butter, cut into 8 pieces
 3 tablespoons honey

1. In a large bowl, combine the flour, sugar, rosemary and salt. Using a pastry blender, cut in butter until mixture resembles coarse crumbs. Using a fork, stir in honey. Knead in bowl until dough begins to cling together. Turn dough out onto a lightly floured surface. Knead dough by folding and gently pressing it for four to six strokes or just until dough holds together. If necessary, cover dough with plastic wrap and chill 30 minutes.

2. On a lightly floured surface, roll dough to ¼-inch thickness. Using 2-inch round cutter, cut into circles. Place 1 inch apart on ungreased large cookie sheet. Reroll as needed.

3. Bake in a 325° oven for 15 to 16 minutes or until edges are firm and tops are lightly browned. Transfer to a wire rack and let cool. **Makes 24 cookies.**

Per cookie: 119 cal, 6 g fat, 15 mg chol, 81 mg sodium, 16 g carbo, 0 g fiber, 1 g pro.

These treats—one an herb-infused butter cookie and the other a jam-filled bite of ethereal coconut—bring a sweet touch to any springtime celebration. They're a perfect fit for a shower, a graduation, Mother's Day or Easter.

Strawberry-Coconut Thumbprints

PREP 45 minutes **CHILL** 1 hour
BAKE 14 minutes per batch
STAND 1 minute per batch

 1 cup butter, softened
 1 3-ounce package cream cheese, softened
 1 cup sugar
 1 egg yolk
 1 tablespoon vanilla
 2½ cups all-purpose flour
 1¼ cups shredded coconut
 ⅓ cup strawberry jam

1. In a large mixing bowl, beat the butter and cream cheese with an electric mixer on medium to high speed for 30 seconds. Add sugar and beat until combined. Add egg yolk and vanilla; beat until combined. Beat in flour. Wrap and chill dough for 1 hour or until easy to handle.

2. Line a cookie sheet with parchment paper; set aside. Shape dough into 1-inch balls. Roll balls in coconut. Arrange 1½ inches apart on prepared cookie sheet. Use thumb to make indentation in each cookie.

3. Bake in a 350° oven about 14 minutes or until edges are light golden. Cool on cookie sheets 1 minute. Use thumb to reimprint cookies. Spoon about ¼ teaspoon jam into center of each. Remove and cool completely on wire racks. **Makes about 48 cookies.**

Per cookie: 103 cal, 6 g fat, 16 mg chol, 42 mg sodium, 12 g carbo, 0 g fiber, 1 g pro.

STRAWBERRY-
COCONUT
THUMBPRINTS

CARAMEL AND
CHOCOLATE KETTLE
CORN CRISPIE BARS

Caramel and Chocolate Kettle Corn Crispie Bars

PREP 30 minutes **COOK** 8 minutes **CHILL** 45 minutes

    8 cups kettle corn
    1 8-ounce package chocolate-covered
        toffee pieces
    1 cup pecans, toasted and finely chopped
    ⅔ cup light-color corn syrup
    ⅔ cup sweetened condensed milk
    ½ cup packed brown sugar
    5 tablespoons butter
    3 tablespoons granulated sugar
    1 teaspoon vanilla
    1 12-ounce package semisweet chocolate
        pieces or one 11.5-ounce package milk
        chocolate pieces, melted*
    ¼ cup caramel ice cream topping (optional)
    2 to 3 teaspoons coarse sea salt

1. Line a 13x9x2-inch baking pan with foil, extending foil over edges of pan; set pan aside. In a very large bowl, toss together the kettle corn, toffee pieces and pecans; set aside.

2. In a small saucepan, combine the corn syrup, condensed milk, brown sugar, butter and granulated sugar. Bring mixture to boiling over medium-high heat, stirring constantly. Reduce heat and boil gently, uncovered, for 6 to 8 minutes or until the caramel sauce is a light golden brown, stirring frequently. Remove from heat; stir in vanilla. Pour caramel sauce over kettle corn mixture, stirring with a wooden spoon until coated. Transfer mixture to prepared pan, pressing firmly into pan using the back of the wooden spoon or a large piece of waxed paper.

3. Spread melted chocolate over kettle corn mixture. If you like, drizzle with caramel topping. Sprinkle with sea salt. Chill for 45 to 60 minutes or until chocolate is set. Use foil to lift kettle corn mixture from pan. Use a sharp knife to cut into bars, wiping blade with wet paper towels between cuts. **Makes 20 servings.**

*Note: To melt chocolate, place chocolate pieces in a large microwave-safe bowl. Heat on 50 percent (medium) power for 2 to 3 minutes or just until chocolate is melted, stirring twice.

Per serving: 297 cal, 17 g fat, 15 mg chol, 258 mg sodium, 37 g carbo, 2 g fiber, 2 g pro.

Go-Anywhere Rhubarb Squares

These squares, which travel well, combine a rhubarb filling with a cookie crust.

PREP 20 minutes **BAKE** 47 minutes

    1 cup all-purpose flour
    ⅓ cup sifted powdered sugar
    ⅓ cup butter
    1 cup granulated sugar
    ¼ cup all-purpose flour
    2 slightly beaten eggs
    1 teaspoon vanilla
    3 cups finely chopped fresh or frozen
        rhubarb*

1. In a mixing bowl, combine the 1 cup flour and the powdered sugar. Cut in butter until mixture resembles coarse crumbs.

2. Pat the crumb mixture into the bottom of an 11x7x1½-inch or 9x9x2-inch baking pan. Bake in a 350° oven for 12 minutes.

3. In the mixing bowl, beat together granulated sugar, the ¼ cup flour, the eggs and vanilla. Stir in rhubarb. Pour over warm crust in baking pan.

4. Bake for 35 minutes more or lightly browned around edges and center is set. Let cool in the pan on a wire rack. Serve warm or cool. Store in the refrigerator. **Makes 16 servings.**

*Note: If using frozen rhubarb, thaw just enough so fruit will chop easily. Then use as directed.

Per serving: 138 cal, 5 g fat, 37 mg chol, 50 mg sodium, 22 g carbo, 1 g fiber, 2 g pro.

Just when you thought kettle corn couldn't get any better, this prizewinning recipe throws chocolate, caramel and toffee into the sweet-salty mix for a crispy treat that is absolutely irresistible.

SUNCREST GARDENS FARM'S
GARDEN DELIGHT, PAGE 85

Summer

APPETIZERS

Devilishly Good Deviled Eggs 61

Fresh Corn and Avocado Pico de Gallo 58

Hamburger Steak Sliders 65

Shrimp and Melon Soup 62

Sinfully Good Deviled Eggs 61

Sweet 'n' Hot Corn and Blueberry Relish 61

BREAKFAST

Breakfast Custard Parfaits with Granola 54

BREADS

Blueberry Muffins 57

Blueberry Streusel Coffee Cake 54

The Stone Barn's Pizza Dough 78

Whole Wheat Pizza Dough 78

BEVERAGES

Lemon-Mint Honeyed Iced Tea 62

Sparkling Berry Lemonade 62

MAIN DISHES

BLT Chicken Sliders 73

Chicken and Corn Hash Brown Bake 73

Fresh Corn Risotto with Wild Rice and Pancetta 69

Fresh Herb Pasta Primavera 82

Fresh Tomato and Arugula Pasta 82

Grilled Sirloin Kabobs with Zesty Top City Sauce 65

Grilled Walleye Pike with Tomato-Basil Sauce 81

Grilled Whole Whitefish 81

Heirloom Tomato and Onion Quiche 90

The Stone Barn's The Alaskan 77

The Stone Barn's The Modena 77

Stuffed Cheesesteaks 66

Summer Corn Chowder 70

Suncrest Gardens Farm's Garden Delight 85

Suncrest Gardens Farm's Pesto Pizza 86

Sweet Corn Pizza 85

Whole Grilled Whitefish 81

SIDES

Cornmeal Griddle Cakes with Sauteed Corn 97

Corn on the Cob with Flavored Butters 98

Grilled Green Tomatoes with Garden Herb Salad 93

Grilled Tomato Melts 101

Grilled Zucchini with Tomatoes 101

Old-Fashioned Scalloped Corn 94

Watermelon, Feta and Mint Salad 93

SWEETS

Blueberry Pound Cake 111

Crispy Cherry-Almond Bars with Marshmallows 115

Easy Peach Ice Cream 115

Finnish Blueberry Pie (Mustikkapiirakka) 105

Kiwi Summer Limeade Pie 109

Mixed Cherry Clafouti 109

North Dakota Juneberry Pie 102

Peach-Brown Butter Tart 106

Peach Kuchen 111

Raspberry Pie 106

Sweet Corn Ice Cream 112

Tropical Berry Pops 115

Uncovered Blueberry Pie 105

Breakfast Custard Parfaits with Granola

START TO FINISH 25 minutes

1½ cups fat-free milk
1 4-serving-size package fat-free sugar-free reduced-calorie vanilla instant pudding mix
¼ cup tub-style fat-free cream cheese
1 tablespoon honey
2 tablespoons orange or clementine juice
1 tablespoon very finely chopped crystallized ginger
2 cups fresh berries (such as raspberries, halved strawberries, blueberries, blackberries and/or black raspberries)
1 cup orange or clementine sections
1 cup low-fat granola
Assorted berries (such as raspberries, halved strawberries, blueberries, blackberries and/or black raspberries; optional)

1. In a medium mixing bowl, stir the milk into pudding mix. Beat with an electric mixer on low speed for 2 minutes; set aside. In a large mixing bowl, beat cream cheese and honey with an electric mixer on medium to high speed for 15 seconds. Beat in the orange juice and crystallized ginger. Gradually add pudding mixture to cream cheese mixture, beating until combined.

2. In six 6- to 8-ounce parfait glasses, layer 1 cup of the berries, ½ cup orange sections, half of the custard mixture and half of the granola. Repeat layers. If you like, garnish with a few additional berries. Serve immediately. **Makes 6 servings.**

Make-ahead tip: Prepare as above except omit granola when layering. Cover and chill up to 24 hours. Top each parfait with granola just before serving.

Per serving: 173 cal, 1 g fat, 2 mg chol, 357 mg sodium, 36 g carbo, 5 g fiber, 6 g pro.

Blueberry Streusel Coffee Cake

A thick layer of juicy blueberries adds moistness to this old-fashioned favorite from The White Gull Inn in Door County, Wisconsin.

PREP 30 minutes **BAKE** 35 minutes

1½ cups packed brown sugar
1 cup coarsely chopped nuts
4 teaspoons ground cinnamon
1 8-ounce carton dairy sour cream
1 teaspoon baking soda
¾ cup granulated sugar
½ cup butter, softened
3 eggs
1 teaspoon vanilla
2 cups all-purpose flour
1½ teaspoons baking powder
2 cups fresh or frozen blueberries, thawed
½ cup powdered sugar
2 teaspoons milk
¼ teaspoon vanilla

1. For topping: In a small bowl, combine brown sugar, nuts and cinnamon. Set aside. In another small bowl, stir together sour cream and baking soda. Set aside. Grease a 13x9x2-inch baking pan. Set aside.

2. In a large mixing bowl, combine granulated sugar and softened butter; beat with an electric mixer on medium speed until well mixed. Beat in eggs and vanilla until well mixed. Add the flour and baking powder; beat until well mixed. Add the foamy sour cream mixture; beat until well mixed.

3. Spread half of the batter into the prepared pan. Sprinkle blueberries over batter. Sprinkle half of the topping over the blueberries. Carefully spread remaining batter over the topping; sprinkle remaining topping over the batter.

4. Bake in 350° oven for 35 to 40 minutes or until a toothpick inserted near the center comes out clean.

5. For icing: In a small bowl, combine powdered sugar, milk, and vanilla. Stir in enough additional milk, 1 teaspoon at a time, to make icing of drizzling consistency. Drizzle cake with icing. Serve cake warm, or cool on a wire rack. **Makes 16 servings.**

Per serving: 345 cal, 14 g fat, 61 mg chol, 184 mg sodium, 51 g carbo, 2 g fiber, 4 g pro.

BLUEBERRY
STREUSEL COFFEE
CAKE

Blueberry Muffins

A basket of warm blueberry muffins on the breakfast table is a siren call to sleepyheads.

PREP 15 minutes **BAKE** 25 minutes
COOL 5 minutes

- 2 cups all-purpose flour
- 2 teaspoons baking powder
- ½ teaspoon salt
- ½ cup butter, softened
- 1 cup sugar
- 2 eggs
- ½ cup milk
- 1 teaspoon vanilla
- 2 to 2½ cups fresh or frozen blueberries
- 1 tablespoon sugar
- ¼ teaspoon ground cinnamon

1. Line sixteen 2½-inch (standard) or six 3½-inch (jumbo) muffin cups with paper bake cups; set aside. In a medium bowl, combine flour, baking powder and salt; set aside.

2. In a large mixing bowl, beat butter with an electric mixer on medium speed for 30 seconds. Add the 1 cup sugar; beat until well combined. Beat in eggs, milk and vanilla (mixture will look slightly curdled). Stir in flour mixture just until moistened (batter should be lumpy). Gently stir in blueberries.

3. Spoon batter into prepared muffin cups, filling each nearly full. In a small bowl, combine the 1 tablespoon sugar and cinnamon. Sprinkle sugar mixture over batter.

4. Bake in a 350° oven for 25 to 30 minutes (standard) or 35 to 40 minutes (jumbo) or until golden and a wooden toothpick inserted in centers comes out clean. Cool in muffin cups on a wire rack for 5 minutes. Remove from muffin cups; serve warm.
Makes 16 standard or 6 jumbo muffins.

Per standard-size serving: 184 cal, 7 g fat, 42 mg chol, 171 mg sodium, 29 g carbo, 1 g fiber, 3 g pro.

Michigan is the country's No.1 producer of highbush blueberries—more than 100 million pounds each year.

Fresh Corn and Avocado Pico de Gallo

This fresh and chunky salsa is a natural with tortilla chips, but it's equally delicious with grilled chicken, steak, pork or fish.

PREP 45 minutes **BROIL** 7 minutes **STAND** 15 minutes **CHILL** 4 to 24 hours

1 fresh poblano or Anaheim chile pepper* or 1 medium green sweet pepper

1 medium red, orange or yellow sweet pepper

2 cups grape and/or cherry tomatoes, halved or quartered, or 4 medium tomatoes, seeded and coarsely chopped (2 cups)

1 cup fresh corn kernels; 1 cup frozen whole kernel corn, thawed, or one 8.75-ounce can whole kernel corn, drained

¼ cup finely chopped red onion or thinly sliced green onion

¼ cup snipped fresh cilantro

½ teaspoon finely shredded lime peel

2 tablespoons lime juice

1 to 2 cloves garlic, minced

1 teaspoon kosher salt or ½ teaspoon salt

⅛ teaspoon bottled hot pepper sauce or ¼ teaspoon freshly ground black pepper

1 avocado, halved, seeded, peeled and chopped

Baked tortilla chips or corn chips

1. Place whole poblano and sweet pepper on a foil-lined baking sheet. Broil 4 inches from the heat for 7 to 10 minutes or until skins are bubbly and blackened, turning occasionally. Carefully bring the foil up and around the peppers to enclose. Let stand about 15 minutes or until cool enough to handle. Pull the skins off gently and slowly using a paring knife. Discard skins. Remove pepper stems, seeds and membranes; discard. Chop the peppers.

2. In a large bowl, combine chopped peppers, tomatoes, corn, red onion, cilantro, lime peel, lime juice, garlic, salt and hot pepper sauce. Cover and chill mixture 4 to 24 hours. Stir in avocado just before serving.

3. Serve with tortilla chips. **Makes 24 (¼ cup) servings.**

*Note: Because hot chile peppers contain volatile oils that can burn your skin and eyes, avoid direct contact with them as much as possible. When working with chile peppers, wear plastic or rubber gloves. If your bare hands do touch the peppers, wash your hands and nails well with soap and warm water.

Per serving: 42 cal, 1 g fat, 0 mg chol, 111 mg sodium, 8 g carbo, 1 g fiber, 1 g pro.

Fresh Corn and Black Bean Pico de Gallo: Prepare as directed, except substitute one 15-ounce can black beans, rinsed and drained, for the avocado.

A well-made salsa is like summer in a bowl—a colorful melange of fresh-from-the-garden sweet corn; ripe, juicy tomatoes; and rich, creamy, buttery avocados spiked with lime and chilies.

SWEET 'N' HOT
CORN BLUEBERRY
RELISH

Sweet 'n' Hot Corn and Blueberry Relish

PREP 25 minutes **CHILL** 4 hours

- 1 tablespoon corn oil or vegetable oil
- 2 cups fresh corn kernels or one 10-ounce package frozen whole kernel corn, thawed (2 cups)
- 1 to 2 cloves garlic, minced
- 2 tomatillos, husks removed, rinsed and finely chopped (about ½ cup)
- 2 fresh jalapeño or serrano chile peppers, seeded and finely chopped (see Note, page 58)
- ¼ cup snipped fresh cilantro
- 3 tablespoons honey
- 1 teaspoon finely shredded lime peel
- 2 tablespoons lime juice
- ¼ teaspoon salt
- 1 cup fresh blueberries

1. In a large nonstick skillet, cook corn and garlic in hot oil over medium heat for 5 minutes. Stir in the tomatillos and jalapeño peppers. Cook and stir about 5 minutes more or until the tomatillos are soft (the corn should be cooked but still firm). Remove from heat and cool slightly. Stir in the cilantro, honey, lime peel, juice and salt.

2. Gently toss in blueberries. Chill in a covered container for 4 hours to allow flavors to blend.

3. Bring relish to room temperature before serving. Serve relish with tortilla chips or as a side dish or with grilled steaks, chops, burgers, chicken or fish. **Makes 10 (½ cup) servings.**

Per serving: 73 cal, 2 g fat, 0 mg chol, 61 mg sodium, 15 g carbo, 1 g fiber, 1 g pro.

Devilishly Good Deviled Eggs

Endlessly versatile and universally appealing, these classic creamy orbs are perfect for any kind of entertaining—from the casual backyard barbecue to an elegant sit-down dinner.

PREP 20 minutes **STAND** 18 minutes

- 8 extra-large eggs
- 3 tablespoons mayonnaise or salad dressing
- 3 tablespoons Mexican crema, sour cream or créme fraîche
- 1 teaspoon finely chopped canned chipotle pepper in adobo sauce
- 1 teaspoon cider vinegar
- ¼ teaspoon curry powder
- ⅛ teaspoon salt
- 3 tablespoons chutney
- Snipped fresh herbs (such as parsley, basil and/or chives; optional)

1. Place eggs in a single layer in a large saucepan. Add enough cold water to cover the eggs by 1 inch. Bring to a rapid boil over high heat. Remove from heat, cover and let stand for 18 minutes; drain.

2. Run cold water over the eggs or place them in ice water until cool enough to handle; drain. To peel eggs, gently tap each egg on the countertop. Roll the egg between the palms of your hands. Peel off eggshell, starting at the large end, under running water. Halve hard-cooked eggs lengthwise and remove yolks. Set whites aside.

3. In a food processor, combine yolks, mayonnaise, Mexican crema, chipotle pepper, vinegar, curry powder and salt, scraping down sides of bowl as necessary. Transfer the filling to a pastry bag with an open star tip (No. 21) or a resealable plastic bag with a small bit of the corner snipped off. Pipe the yolk mixture into egg white halves. Transfer eggs to a serving platter. Cover and chill until serving time (up to 24 hours).

4. To serve, snip any large pieces of chutney. Garnish each egg half with a little of the chutney. If you like, sprinkle eggs and platter with snipped fresh herbs. **Makes 16 servings.**

Sinfully Good Deviled Eggs: Prepare as directed, except omit chipotle pepper and chutney. Stir in 1 tablespoon smoked oysters or smoked trout, rinsed, drained and finely chopped. Garnish each with a sprinkle of smoked paprika.

Per serving: 76 cal, 6 g fat, 134 mg chol, 104 mg sodium, 2 g carbo, 0 g fiber, 4 g pro.

Shrimp and Melon Soup

PREP 30 minutes **CHILL** 2 hours

  1 pound fresh or frozen small cold-water
     shrimp (Northern pink shrimp), peeled
     and deveined
  ¼ teaspoon salt
  ⅛ teaspoon freshly ground black pepper
  1 very ripe medium crenshaw (golden
     honeydew melon), Persian melon or
     cantaloupe, peeled, seeded and cubed
     (about 6 cups)
  ½ cup dairy sour cream or plain yogurt
  1 tablespoon grated fresh ginger
     Snipped fresh cilantro or Italian (flat-leaf)
     parsley (optional)
     Sour cream or plain yogurt (optional)
     Cooked shrimp (optional)

1. Thaw shrimp, if frozen. Rinse shrimp. Sprinkle with salt and pepper. In a large saucepan, cook shrimp, uncovered, in just enough boiling water to cover for about 1 minute or until shrimp are opaque; drain.

2. In a food processor bowl or blender container, combine half of the shrimp with half of the melon, half of the sour cream and half of the ginger. Cover and process or blend until smooth. Transfer to a large bowl. Repeat with remaining shrimp, melon, sour cream and ginger. Stir into mixture in bowl.

3. Cover and chill in refrigerator for 2 to 24 hours. Meanwhile, chill soup bowls. To serve, ladle the chilled soup into chilled bowls. If you like, garnish each serving with cilantro, a small dollop of additional sour cream and/or additional cooked shrimp. **Makes 8 (⅔ cup) servings.**

Per serving: 118 cal, 3 g fat, 70 mg chol, 155 mg sodium, 13 g carbo, 1 g fiber, 10 g pro.

Sparkling Berry Lemonade

START TO FINISH 20 minutes

  2 cups fresh or frozen unsweetened berries
     (such as raspberries, sliced strawberries,
     blackberries and/or black raspberries)
  2 cups water
  1 12-ounce can frozen pink lemonade,
     lemonade or limeade concentrate,
     thawed
  2 tablespoons sugar
  1 1-liter bottle club soda, chilled
     Ice cubes
     Lemon and/or lime slices
     Fresh berries (such as raspberries, sliced
     strawberries, blackberries and/or black
     raspberries; optional)

1. In a blender, combine the 2 cups berries and the water. Cover and blend until mixture is pureed. Press mixture through a fine-mesh sieve set over a bowl, forcing puree through with back of spoon or rubber spatula; discard seeds. Pour puree into a 2-quart pitcher. Stir in lemonade concentrate and sugar, stirring until sugar dissolves. Chill lemonade until ready to serve.

2. Before serving, stir lemonade. Slowly pour club soda into lemonade in pitcher. Pour into ice-filled glasses and serve. Garnish each glass with lemon slices and, if you like, additional fresh berries. **Makes 10 (6 ounce) servings.**

Per serving: 84 cal, 0 g fat, 0 mg chol, 24 mg sodium, 22 g carbo, 2 g fiber, 0 g pro.

Lemon-Mint Honeyed Iced Tea

PREP 5 minutes **STAND** 10 minutes
COOL 30 minutes **CHILL** 3 hours

  4 cups water
  4 bags green or black tea
  1 bag mint tea
  ½ of a 12-ounce can (¾ cup) frozen
     lemonade or limeade concentrate,
     thawed
  ⅓ cup honey
     Ice cubes
     Fresh mint leaves or mint sprigs
     Lemon slices or thin wedges

1. In a medium saucepan, bring the water to boiling. Remove from heat. Add tea bags. Cover and let stand for 10 minutes. Remove and discard tea bags. Stir in lemonade concentrate and honey, stirring until honey is dissolved. Cool for 30 minutes.

2. Transfer tea to a 1½-quart pitcher. Cover; chill for at least 3 hours.

3. To serve, pour tea over ice cubes in tall glasses. Garnish with mint leaves and lemon slices. Chill remaining tea for up to 2 days. **Makes 6 servings.**

Per serving: 114 cal, 0 g fat, 0 mg chol, 8 mg sodium, 31 g carbo, 1 g fiber, 1 g pro.

**LEMON-MINT
HONEYED ICED TEA**

HAMBURGER
STEAK SLIDERS

Hamburger Steak Sliders

Serve these 1-ounce burgers as part of an appetizer spread or in multiples as a full meal.

PREP 25 minutes **GRILL** 8 minutes

- ½ cup very finely chopped red onion, green onions, onion, leek or shallots
- ¼ cup beef broth or water
- 2 tablespoons snipped fresh Italian (flat-leaf) parsley (optional)
- 2 tablespoons steak sauce or barbecue sauce or 1 tablespoon Worcestershire sauce
- 1 tablespoon Dijon-style or coarse-grain mustard
- ½ teaspoon freshly ground black pepper
- 12 ounces ground beef sirloin (90 percent lean)
- 12 ounces ground beef chuck (85 percent lean)
- 12 whole grain cocktail-size hamburger buns or small round dinner rolls, split
  Assorted spreads (such as barbecue sauce, steak sauce, ketchup, Dijon-style mustard, coarse-grain mustard, yellow mustard and/or mayonnaise)
  Assorted toppers (such as mini cheddar or Swiss cheese slices; roma tomato slices; torn Bibb, leaf or iceberg lettuce; fresh basil leaves; 2-inch pieces of crisp-cooked bacon; sliced red onion; pickle relish; sweet pickle slices; and/or baby kosher dill pickles; optional)

1. In a large bowl, combine onion; broth; parsley, if you like; steak sauce; mustard; and pepper. Add ground sirloin and chuck; lightly mix together just until combined (do not overmix). Divide meat mixture into 12 portions and shape into round or square ½-inch-thick patties.

2. For a charcoal grill: Grill patties on the greased rack of an uncovered grill directly over medium coals for 8 to 10 minutes or until done (160°), turning once halfway through grilling. Wrap buns in heavy foil and add to grill rack the last 5 minutes of grilling, turning once. (For a gas grill: Preheat grill. Reduce heat to medium. Add patties and buns to grill rack. Cover and grill as above.)*

3. To serve, place burgers in buns. Serve with assorted spreads. If you like, garnish with assorted toppers. **Makes 12 appetizer servings.**

*Note: Or preheat broiler. Place meat patties on the rack of a broiler pan. Broil 3 to 4 inches from the heat for 8 to 10 minutes or until done (160°), turning once halfway through broiling.

Per serving: 193 cal, 8 g fat, 38 mg chol, 269 mg sodium, 16 g carbo, 2 g fiber, 14 g pro.

Grilled Sirloin Kabobs with Zesty Top City Sauce

PREP 30 minutes **GRILL** 8 minutes

- 2 pounds top sirloin steak
- 1 tablespoon dried minced onion
- 2 teaspoons dried chives
- 1 teaspoon kosher salt
- 1 teaspoon dried parsley
- 1 teaspoon smoked paprika
- 1 teaspoon ground black pepper
- 1 recipe Zesty Top City Dipping Sauce (recipe follows)
  Snipped fresh chives (optional)

1. Trim fat from meat. Cut meat into 1-inch pieces. In a small bowl, combine onion, dried chives, salt, parsley, paprika and pepper. Toss meat with seasoning mixture to coat. Thread meat on eight 12-inch metal skewers, leaving ¼ inch between pieces.

2. For a charcoal grill: Grill kabobs on the rack of an uncovered grill directly over medium coals for 8 to 10 minutes or until meat reaches desired doneness, turning once halfway through grilling. (For a gas grill: Preheat grill. Reduce heat to medium. Place kabobs on grill rack over heat. Cover and grill as directed.)

3. Serve sirloin kabobs with Zesty Top City Dipping Sauce. If you like, garnish with fresh chives. **Makes 4 servings.**

Zesty Top City Dipping Sauce: In a small bowl, combine ⅓ cup mayonnaise, ¼ cup chopped oil-packed dried tomatoes, 3 tablespoons sour cream, 2 tablespoons prepared horseradish, 1 teaspoon dried parsley and 1 teaspoon Worcestershire sauce. Cover and chill.

Per serving: 629 cal, 46 g fat, 118 mg chol, 764 mg sodium, 4 g carbo, 1 g fiber, 47 g pro.

Stuffed Cheesesteaks

The secret to this amazingly cheesy grilled steak sandwich is the seasonings, including a little chocolate, cinnamon and allspice. Although the original recipe serves four, it can easily serve eight people if you want to keep the calories and fat in check.

PREP 45 minutes **GRILL** 14 minutes **STAND** 10 minutes

1 onion, cut into ¼-inch slices
  Olive oil
1 fresh portobello mushroom cap (about 4 ounces)
1 red or green sweet pepper or poblano chile pepper, stemmed, seeded and quartered
2 teaspoons chili powder
1 teaspoon salt
1 teaspoon garlic powder
1 teaspoon smoked paprika
1 teaspoon ground cumin
1 teaspoon ground cinnamon
1 teaspoon grated bittersweet chocolate
½ teaspoon ground allspice
½ teaspoon freshly ground black pepper
¼ teaspoon cayenne pepper
2 boneless beef ribeye steaks, cut 1 inch thick (12 to 16 ounces each) and trimmed
8 slices aged provolone cheese (about 5 ounces)
4 hoagie buns, split
2 tablespoons butter, softened

1. Thread onion slices onto metal skewers (like lollipops). Brush both sides of slices with olive oil.

2. Grill onion kabobs, mushroom cap (gill side down) and the pepper quarters on the rack of an uncovered gas grill or uncovered charcoal grill directly over medium heat for 6 to 10 minutes or just until vegetables are tender, turning once halfway through grilling. Remove from grill; cool.

3. Meanwhile, in a small bowl, stir together chili powder, salt, garlic powder, paprika, cumin, cinnamon, bittersweet chocolate, allspice, black pepper and cayenne pepper; set aside.

4. Make a lengthwise cut into the side of each steak, cutting to, but not through, the opposite side (it will open like a book). Brush the outsides of the steaks with olive oil; sprinkle the insides and outsides of steaks with the seasoning mixture.

5. When vegetables are cool enough to handle, remove onion slices from skewers. Cut the grilled onion slices in half. Cut the mushroom and pepper into thin strips.

6. With the first steak "opened," place two slices of cheese on bottom half of steak, staggering the slices so they cover the surface. Layer with half of the vegetables and two more slices of cheese. Close the top half of the steak over cheese and vegetables. Tie together at 2-inch intervals with kitchen string. Repeat with the remaining steak, cheese and vegetables.

7. Place stuffed steaks on the grill. Grill for 14 to 16 minutes or until desired doneness, turning once halfway through grilling. Remove steaks from grill. Let stand, covered, for 10 minutes.

8. Brush the cut sides of the buns with butter. Place buns, cut sides down, on the grill. Grill for 1 to 2 minutes or until lightly toasted.

9. Remove strings from steaks. Slice the stuffed steaks across the grain into ½-inch slices. Divide the stuffed steak slices evenly among toasted buns. **Makes 4 servings.**

Per serving: 1,030 cal, 65 g fat, 165 mg chol, 1,733 mg sodium, 60 g carbo, 5 g fiber, 52 g pro.

Fresh Corn Risotto with Wild Rice and Pancetta

The high starch content of short, fat arborio rice grains helps create the creamy texture that makes risotto so irresistible. It doesn't get much better than this: a silky risotto cooked in butter and bacon drippings and topped with crisp-cooked bacon.

START TO FINISH 55 minutes

8 ounces pancetta, chopped
2 tablespoons butter
2 tablespoons olive oil
1 large onion, finely chopped (1 cup)
1¼ cups uncooked arborio rice
1 cup dry white wine or chicken broth
¼ to ½ teaspoon crushed red pepper
2 14-ounce cans reduced-sodium chicken broth
1½ cups fresh corn kernels or frozen whole kernel corn, thawed
1 cup cooked wild rice*
½ cup freshly grated Parmigiano-Reggiano cheese (2 ounces)
2 tablespoons butter, cut into pieces
½ teaspoon freshly ground black pepper
Shaved Parmigiano-Reggiano cheese
Snipped fresh Italian (flat-leaf) parsley

1. In a large saucepan, cook pancetta in 2 tablespoons butter and the oil over medium-high heat for about 8 minutes or until nicely browned. Using a slotted spoon, remove pancetta and drain on paper towels, reserving drippings in pan. Reduce heat to medium. Add onion to reserved drippings; cook and stir until onion is tender.

2. Add rice to onion mixture in saucepan; cook and stir over medium heat about 3 minutes or until rice begins to brown. Stir in half of the cooked pancetta. Carefully add wine and crushed red pepper.

3. In a medium saucepan, bring broth to boiling; reduce heat and simmer. Slowly add 1 cup of the broth to the rice mixture, stirring constantly. Continue to cook and stir over medium heat until liquid is absorbed. Add another ½ cup of the broth to the rice mixture, stirring constantly until the liquid is absorbed. Add remaining broth mixture, ½ cup at a time, cooking and stirring constantly just until rice is tender and the broth has been absorbed. (This should take about 20 minutes total.)

4. Stir in corn, cooked wild rice, the ½ cup cheese, the butter pieces and black pepper. Cook over low heat for 3 minutes, stirring occasionally.

5. Divide risotto among six shallow pasta dishes or bowls. Sprinkle risotto with the remaining cooked pancetta, shaved cheese and parsley. **Makes 6 to 12 servings.**

*Note: To cook wild rice, rinse ½ cup wild rice, lifting the rice with your fingers to clean thoroughly; drain. In a small saucepan, combine wild rice and 1 cup water. Bring to boiling; reduce heat. Cover and simmer about 40 minutes, without stirring, or until rice is tender and most of the liquid is absorbed. If needed, drain. Makes about 1¼ cups.

Per serving: 559 cal, 28 g fat, 54 mg chol, 1,239 mg sodium, 55 g carbo, 3 g fiber, 18 g pro.

Summer Corn Chowder

START TO FINISH 45 minutes

2 cups fresh corn kernels or one 10-ounce
    package frozen whole kernel corn
    (2 cups)
1 14-ounce can vegetable broth
1 12-ounce package frozen shelled sweet
    soybeans (edamame) or one 10-ounce
    package frozen baby sweet peas
1 large onion, chopped (1 cup)
2 teaspoons snipped fresh marjoram or
    oregano or ¾ teaspoon dried marjoram
    or oregano, crushed
½ teaspoon salt
¼ to ½ teaspoon ground white or black
    pepper
1 14.75-ounce can no-salt-added cream-
    style corn
1 cup cubed lean cooked ham or cooked
    turkey ham
⅔ cup fat-free milk
1 teaspoon Worcestershire sauce
    Fresh marjoram or oregano sprigs
    (optional)

1. In a large saucepan, bring fresh or frozen corn, broth, edamame, onion, marjoram, salt and white pepper to boiling; reduce heat. Simmer, covered, for 5 to 7 minutes or until corn and onion are tender. Stir in undrained cream-style corn, ham, milk and Worcestershire sauce. Heat through.

2. If you like, garnish each serving with a fresh marjoram sprig. **Makes 6 (1⅓ cup) servings.**

Tuna Corn Chowder: Prepare as directed above except omit ham. Stir in one 6-ounce can tuna, drained and broken into chunks, with cream-style corn.

Per serving: 211 cal, 5 g fat, 11 mg chol, 736 mg sodium, 30 g carbo, 5 g fiber, 14 g pro.

Garden-fresh corn—whether enjoyed on the cob slathered in butter with a sprinkle of salt or stirred into a chunky chowder— is one of summer's sweetest pleasures.

**BLT CHICKEN
SLIDERS**

BLT Chicken Sliders

These bitty burgers are topped with sharp white cheddar and a quick-to-fix homemade cranberry ketchup.

PREP 45 minutes **GRILL** 12 minutes

- ½ cup packed brown sugar
- ½ cup coarsely chopped fresh or frozen cranberries
- 3 tablespoons spicy brown mustard
- 3 tablespoons ketchup
- 2½ tablespoons full-flavor molasses
- 1½ teaspoons Worcestershire sauce
- ⅛ teaspoon chili powder
- ⅛ teaspoon sweet smoked paprika
- 12 slices applewood smoked bacon
- 2 tablespoons pure maple syrup
- ½ teaspoon cracked black pepper
- 1¾ pounds uncooked ground skinless, boneless chicken thighs*
- ½ cup finely chopped shallots
- ¼ cup snipped fresh basil
- 1¼ teaspoons salt
- 1 teaspoon snipped fresh thyme
- 2 cloves garlic, minced
- ¼ teaspoon dried sage, crushed
- 1 cup shredded sharp white cheddar cheese (4 ounces)
- 12 small butterhead (Boston or Bibb) lettuce leaves
- 12 small bakery slider rolls or mini buns, split and toasted
- 12 slices roma tomatoes

1. For cranberry ketchup: In a small saucepan, combine brown sugar, cranberries, mustard, ketchup, molasses, Worcestershire sauce, chili powder and paprika. Bring to boiling over medium-high heat, stirring constantly. Reduce heat and boil gently, uncovered, about 10 minutes or until thickened, stirring occasionally. Remove from heat; cover and set aside.

2. In a very large skillet, cook bacon over medium heat until crisp. Stir together maple syrup and pepper. Drizzle over bacon slices in skillet. Cook, covered, for 1 to 2 minutes more. Remove bacon from skillet. Cut bacon slices in half crosswise and wrap in foil.

3. In a large bowl, combine the ground chicken, shallots, basil, salt, thyme, garlic and sage; mix well. Shape into 12 patties.

4. Place patties on a greased rack of a gas or charcoal grill directly over medium heat; grill for 12 to 14 minutes or until no longer pink (165°), turning once. During the last 2 minutes, add the bacon packet to the grill and top patties with cheese.

5. To assemble, place a lettuce leaf on each roll bottom. Top with a tomato slice and two pieces of bacon. Top with a burger and a spoonful of cranberry ketchup. Add roll tops. **Makes 12 sliders.**

*Note: Have a butcher grind skinless, boneless chicken thighs for you.

Per slider: 327 cal, 11 g fat, 73 mg chol, 746 mg sodium, 33 g carbo, 1 g fiber, 22 g pro.

Chicken and Corn Hash Brown Bake

PREP 25 minutes **BAKE** 1 hour 20 minutes
STAND 10 minutes

- 1 10.75-ounce can reduced-fat and reduced-sodium condensed cream of chicken soup
- 1 8-ounce carton dairy sour cream
- ½ cup milk
- 2 teaspoons dried dillweed or dried basil, crushed
- ¾ teaspoon ground black pepper
- 1 28-ounce package frozen diced hash brown potatoes with onions and peppers, thawed
- 2 cups chopped smoked or roasted chicken or turkey
- 2 cups fresh sweet corn kernels, one 10-ounce package frozen whole kernel corn, thawed (2 cups), or one 15.25-ounce can whole kernel corn, drained
- 1 8-ounce package cream cheese, cut into cubes
- 1 8-ounce package shredded Colby, cheddar or Swiss cheese (2 cups)
- 1 cup seasoned croutons, coarsely crushed (optional)

1. In a very large bowl, combine soup, sour cream, milk, dill and pepper. Stir in hash browns, chicken, corn, cream cheese and ½ cup of the Colby cheese. Spoon mixture into a greased 13x9x2-inch baking dish (3-quart rectangular).

2. Bake, covered, in a 350° oven for 40 minutes. Uncover and stir mixture. Sprinkle with the remaining 1½ cups cheese. Bake, uncovered, about 40 minutes more or until top is golden and potatoes are tender, sprinkling with croutons, if you like, the last 10 minutes of baking. Let stand 10 minutes before serving. **Makes 12 servings.**

Per serving: 310 cal, 18 g fat, 64 mg chol, 715 mg sodium, 25 g carbo, 2 g fiber, 15 g pro.

The Stone Barn pizza restaurant in western Wisconsin features a wood-fired oven and a gorgeous courtyard in back in which to sit and enjoy the fresh fare. The pizzas feature locally grown ingredients—often, the vegetables and herbs are grown right on the farm.

THE STONE BARN'S
THE MODENA

The Stone Barn's The Modena

The name Modena refers to the town in Italy that is home to balsamic vinegar, which gives the marinade for the chicken on this pizza its characteristic sweetness and depth of flavor.

PREP 2O minutes **MARINATE** 2O minutes **BAKE** 2O minutes **COOL** 5 minutes

½ cup Balsamic Marinade (recipe follows)
3 cups cooked chicken, cut into ½-inch cubes
2 tablespoons olive oil
2 cloves garlic, minced
   The Stone Barn's Pizza Dough (see page 78) or desired crusts
¾ cup finely chopped Vidalia onion or other sweet onion
3 cups sliced fresh mushrooms, sauteed*
¾ cup trimmed and coarsely chopped fresh sugar snap peas or asparagus
¾ cup crumbled feta cheese (3 ounces)

1. Prepare Balsamic Marinade. In a bowl, combine chicken and Balsamic Marinade. Marinate at room temperature for 20 minutes; drain. Meanwhile, in a small bowl, combine olive oil and garlic; set aside.

2. As directed in Step 7 of The Stone Barn's Pizza Dough recipe (page 78), bake pizza crusts in a 450° oven for 12 minutes or until crusts are light brown before adding toppings. Remove from oven. Or grill pizza using the method in Pizza on the Grill (see Whole Wheat Pizza Dough recipe, page 78). Drain chicken, discarding marinade.

3. For each pizza, lightly coat top of crust with one-third of the garlic-olive oil, spreading to the edges of the crust. Top with one-third of the chicken, onion, mushrooms and sugar snap peas. Sprinkle each with feta cheese.

4. Bake for 8 minutes more or until crust bottom is crisp and brown. (Or grill as directed.) Remove from oven. Cool on baking sheets on wire racks for 5 minutes. **Makes 12 (2-wedge servings).**

Balsamic Marinade: In a medium bowl, combine ½ cup balsamic vinegar; 2 to 3 garlic cloves, minced; 1 tablespoon Dijon-style mustard; ¼ teaspoon salt; and ¼ teaspoon freshly ground black pepper. Using a wire whisk, slowly add 1½ cups olive oil in a thin, steady stream, whisking continually (mixture will thicken as you whisk). Makes 2 cups.

*Note: Saute mushrooms in 2 tablespoons hot olive oil in a 12-inch skillet over medium-high heat. Cook and stir for 6 to 8 minutes or until mushrooms are tender and browned and most of the liquid has evaporated.

Per serving: 347 cal, 18 g fat, 39 mg chol, 546 mg sodium, 30 g carbo, 2 g fiber, 17 g pro.

The Stone Barn's The Alaskan

Bagels and lox were the inspiration for this unusual pizza. (Leftovers are good served cold for breakfast.)

PREP 35 minutes **BAKE** 2O minutes
COOL 5 minutes

1 8-ounce package cream cheese, softened
¼ cup water
   The Stone Barn's Pizza Dough (see page 78) or desired pizza crust
⅓ cup capers, drained
3 tablespoons snipped fresh dill or 1½ teaspoons dried dillweed
8 ounces thinly sliced smoked salmon (lox-style), cut into ½-inch strips
1 cup chopped Vidalia onion or other sweet onion

1. In a small bowl, combine cream cheese and the water, whisking until smooth and spreadable. Set aside.

2. For each pizza, spread top of dough evenly with one-third of the cream cheese mixture, spreading to the edges. Sprinkle each with one-third of the dill. Top with one-third of the capers, salmon and onion.

3. Bake in a 450° oven for 20 to 25 minutes or until toppings are heated through and crust bottom is crisp and brown. (Or grill as directed in Pizza on the Grill in Whole Wheat Pizza Dough recipe, page 78.) Remove from oven. Cool in pans on a wire rack for 5 minutes. Cut into wedges to serve. **Makes 12 (2-wedge) servings.**

Per serving: 233 cal, 9 g fat, 25 mg chol, 942 mg sodium, 29 g carbo, 1 g fiber, 9 g pro.

The Stone Barn's Pizza Dough

PREP 25 minutes **RISE** 2 hours **BAKE** 20 minutes
STAND 15 minutes **COOL** 5 minutes

1¼ cups warm water (105°)
 1 teaspoon active dry yeast (about half of a
    package)
 3 cups bread flour
 2 teaspoons salt
 1 tablespoon olive oil
    Cornmeal

1. In a large mixing bowl, combine the water and yeast. Let stand for 5 minutes. Stir yeast mixture to make sure yeast has dissolved. Meanwhile, in a medium bowl, combine 1½ cups of the bread flour and salt. Add flour mixture and oil to the yeast mixture. Beat with an electric mixer on low speed for 1 minute. Beat on medium speed for 5 minutes more. Stir in remaining flour.

2. Turn dough out onto a lightly floured surface. Knead dough only a couple of strokes; dough will be sticky. Shape dough into a ball. Place dough in a lightly greased bowl, turning once to grease dough surface. Cover bowl; let dough rise in a warm place for 2 hours (dough will not double in size).

3. Grease three large baking sheets. Sprinkle pans lightly with cornmeal. Set aside.

4. Turn dough out onto a floured surface. Cut dough into three equal parts with a serrated knife. Cover; let rest for 10 minutes.

5. Pat each piece of dough into a disk. On a well-floured surface, roll out each dough portion to a very thin 13-inch circle in diameter (don't worry if pizza isn't perfectly round). For a thicker crust, roll out each dough portion into a 11-inch circle. Transfer dough circles to prepared pans.

6. Prick dough all over with a fork. (Do not let rise. If all three pans do not fit in your oven for prebaking, chill one of the pans in the refrigerator.)

7. Bake in a 450° oven for 12 minutes or until crust bottom is light brown. Remove from oven. Add toppings as directed in pizza recipe. **Makes 12 (2-wedge serving) servings.**

Per serving: 140 cal, 2 g fat, 0 mg chol, 389 mg sodium, 27 g carbo, 1 g fiber, 4 g pro.

Whole Wheat Pizza Dough

PREP 30 minutes **RISE** 1 hour 5 minutes

 2 cups all-purpose flour
 ¼ cup quick-cooking polenta, corn grits or
    cornmeal
 1 package active dry yeast
 2 teaspoons sugar
 ¾ teaspoon salt
 ¼ teaspoon ground black pepper
1¼ cups warm water (120° to 130°)
 3 tablespoons olive oil
 1 egg
1½ to 2 cups whole wheat flour
    Polenta, corn grits or cornmeal
    Olive oil

1. In a large mixing bowl, combine the all-purpose flour, the ¼ cup polenta, yeast, sugar, salt and pepper; add the warm water, oil and egg. Beat with an electric mixer on low speed for 30 seconds, scraping bowl. Beat on high speed for 3 minutes. Using a wooden spoon, stir in as much of the whole wheat flour as you can.

2. Turn dough out onto a lightly floured surface. Knead in enough of the remaining ½ cup whole wheat flour to make a moderately stiff dough that is smooth and elastic (6 to 8 minutes), adding additional flour as needed to keep dough from sticking. Place dough in a lightly greased bowl, turning once to grease dough surface. Cover bowl with a damp towel (make sure the towel does not touch the dough). Let dough rise in a warm place until double in size (45 to 55 minutes).

3. Grease three 12- to 14-inch pizza pans, three large baking sheets or one 16x12x1-inch baking pan.* Sprinkle pan(s) with additional polenta. Set aside.

4. Punch down dough. Turn dough out onto a lightly floured surface. If doing three pizzas, cut dough into three equal parts with a serrated knife (about 11 ounces each). Cover; let rest for 10 minutes. Pat each piece of dough into a disk.*

5. On a lightly floured surface, roll out each dough portion to a very thin, 13- to 15-inch circle (don't worry if pizza isn't perfectly round). For a thicker crust, roll out each dough portion into a 11-inch circle. Transfer dough circles to prepared pans. (If using 16x12x1-inch baking pan, roll dough into 16x12-inch rectangle and place in prepared pan.) Build up edges slightly. Cover dough with a damp towel and let rise for 20 minutes.

6. Prick dough all over with a fork. Lightly brush top(s) with additional olive oil. Proceed as directed in pizza recipe.
Makes 12 (2-wedge serving) servings.

*Note: To bake pizzas on a round baking stone or tile, place unheated pizza stone on the middle rack in an unheated oven. Preheat oven to 450°. Roll a portion of Whole Wheat Pizza Dough as directed on a flat baking sheet or pizza peel sprinkled with cornmeal. Prick crust all over with a fork. Gently slide the crust onto hot baking stone. Or with a quick jerk of your arms, carefully slide the crust off prepared baking sheet or peel onto hot baking stone. Bake for 8 to 10 minutes or until crust is light brown.

Per serving: 208 cal, 5 g fat, 18 mg chol, 153 mg sodium, 35 g carbo, 3 g fiber, 6 g pro.

Frozen Bread Dough Pizza Crust: Use a 1-pound loaf frozen whole wheat or white bread dough, thawed. Cut dough into three equal parts with a serrated knife. Roll out and proceed as directed in Whole Wheat Pizza Dough. Makes three 12- to 14-inch pizzas.

Bread Machine Pizza Dough: Whole Wheat Pizza Dough can be made using a bread machine, adding the liquid ingredients (water, oil and egg), dry ingredients next (all purpose flour, whole wheat flour, polenta, sugar, salt and pepper) and yeast last. Put the machine on the Dough setting. Add additional liquid or flour as needed to make a moderately stiff dough. Makes three 12- to 14-inch pizzas.

Pizza on the Grill: To grill pizza dough., prepare the dough as directed. Cut dough into six equal parts with a serrated knife. Cover; let rest for 10 minutes. On two or three very large greased baking sheets sprinkled with cornmeal, roll each dough portion into a 9-inch circle (don't worry if pizza isn't perfectly round). Add more cornmeal as needed. Separating each pizza dough circle with sheets of waxed paper, stack the circles on a waxed paper-lined baking sheet. Wrap and freeze dough about 30 minutes or until firm. Remove pizza dough circles from freezer, discarding waxed paper, and brush tops with some olive oil.

For charcoal grill: Carefully slide two of the pizza dough circles, oiled sides down, onto a lightly oiled rack of an uncovered grill directly over medium-hot coals. Grill for 1 to 2 minutes or until dough is puffed in some places and underside is starting to become firm and crisp. Carefully turn the crusts with long-handled tongs or spatula, transferring them from rack to the back of a baking sheet. Working quickly and carefully, brush oil over grilled top of crust. Add shredded cheese, then add desired toppings to each pizza crust. Transfer the pizzas from the baking sheet to the rack. Grill for 1 to 2 minutes more or until ingredients are hot, cheese is bubbly and bottom crust is crisp and brown. Remove from grill; transfer pizzas to a cutting board. Repeat grilling with remaining four dough portions and toppings. Cut into wedges to serve. Serve immediately. (For a gas grill: Preheat grill. Reduce heat to medium-hot. Place dough circles on grill rack over heat. Cover and grill as above.)

Fresh ingredients and wood-fired ovens make the "pizza farms" of western Wisconsin popular draws on summer weekends. Visitors enjoy delicious food in beautiful and bucolic settings.

GRILLED WHOLE
WHITEFISH

Grilled Whole Whitefish

PREP 20 minutes **GRILL** 35 minutes

- 1 2½- to 3¼-pound dressed fresh or frozen whitefish, pike, cod, tilefish, rockfish, sea trout or orange roughy (scaled, with head and tail intact)
  Salt and freshly ground black pepper
- 1 lemon, thinly sliced and seeded
- 2 sprigs fresh thyme
- 3 cups cooked brown rice
- 1 large onion, chopped
- 1 large tomato, chopped
- 2 tablespoons snipped fresh basil or
  1 teaspoon dried basil, crushed
- ¼ teaspoon salt
- ¼ teaspoon freshly ground black pepper
  Lemon wedges (optional)
  Thyme sprigs (optional)

1. Thaw fish, if frozen. Rinse fish; pat dry. (If you like, remove head and tail.) Lightly grease a 24x18-inch piece of heavy-duty foil. Place fish on foil. Open fish and season cavity lightly with salt and black pepper. Arrange half of the sliced lemon and a thyme sprig in cavity.

2. Close fish. Top with remaining lemon slices and thyme sprig. Bring up two opposite edges of foil and seal with a double fold. Fold remaining edges together to completely enclose fish, leaving space for steam to build.

3. In a medium bowl, combine rice, onion, tomato, basil, ¼ teaspoon salt and ¼ teaspoon pepper. Tear off a 36x18-inch piece of heavy-duty foil; fold in half to make an 18-inch square. Place rice mixture in center of square. Bring up two opposite edges of foil and seal with a double fold. Fold remaining edges together to completely enclose rice, leaving space for steam to build.

4. For a charcoal grill: Arrange medium-hot coals around edges of grill. Test for medium heat in center of grill. Place fish in center of grill rack. Cover and grill for 10 minutes. Add rice packet next to fish but not over coals. Grill 25 to 35 minutes more or until fish flakes easily when tested with a fork and rice is heated through. (For a gas grill: Preheat grill. Reduce heat to medium. Adjust for indirect cooking. Grill as above.)

5. Use two large spatulas to transfer foil packet from grill to a large serving platter. Serve fish with rice mixture. Garnish with lemon wedges and additional fresh thyme sprigs, if you like. **Makes 6 servings.**

Per serving: 372 cal, 11 g fat, 109 mg chol, 249 mg sodium, 27 g carbo, 3 g fiber, 39 g pro.

Grilled Walleye Pike with Tomato-Basil Sauce

PREP 10 minutes **GRILL** 6 minutes

- 2 pounds fresh walleye pike or catfish fillets, about ½ to ¾ inch thick
- 1 tablespoon canola or cooking oil
  Salt and ground black pepper
- 2 tablespoons unsalted butter or butter
- 1 large tomato, peeled, seeded and finely chopped (¾ cup)
- ¼ cup water
- 1 tablespoon lemon juice
- ⅛ teaspoon ground white pepper
- 2 tablespoons snipped fresh basil

1. Brush fish with canola oil. Season fish with salt and ground black pepper. Place fillets in a greased grill basket. For a charcoal grill: Place grill basket on grill rack directly over medium coals for 6 to 9 minutes or until fish flakes easily when tested with a fork. (For a gas grill, preheat grill. Reduce heat to medium. Place grill basket on grill rack over heat. Cover and grill as above.)

2. Meanwhile, for the sauce, cook the butter and tomato over medium heat until butter has just melted. Stir in the water, lemon juice and white pepper; remove from heat. Set aside.

3. Just before serving, stir basil into sauce. Top each fillet with a spoonful of sauce. **Makes 6 to 8 servings.**

Per serving: 202 cal, 8 g fat, 141 mg chol, 129 mg sodium, 1 g carbo, 0 g fiber, 29 g pro.

Fresh Tomato and Arugula Pasta

START TO FINISH 30 minutes

2⅔ cups dried ziti or mostaccioli (8 ounces)
 1 medium onion, thinly sliced
 2 cloves garlic, minced
 1 tablespoon olive oil
 4 to 6 medium tomatoes, seeded and coarsely chopped (3 cups)
 ½ teaspoon salt
 ¼ teaspoon black pepper
 ⅛ to ¼ teaspoon crushed red pepper (optional)
 4 cups arugula and/or spinach, coarsely chopped
 ¼ cup pine nuts or slivered almonds, toasted
 ¼ cup crumbled Gorgonzola or Parmesan cheese

1. Cook pasta according to package directions. Drain; keep warm.

2. Meanwhile, in a large skillet, cook onion and garlic in hot olive oil over medium heat until onion is tender. Add tomatoes, salt, black pepper, and, if desired, red pepper. Cook and stir over medium-high heat about 2 minutes or until the tomatoes are warm and release some of their juices. Stir in arugula; heat just until greens are wilted.

3. To serve, top pasta with tomato mixture; sprinkle with toasted pine nuts and cheese. **Makes 4 (1¼ cup) servings.**

Fresh Tomato and Arugula Pasta with Chicken: Prepare as above except stir 2 cups chopped deli-roasted chicken into tomato mixture along with arugula.

Per serving: 362 cal, 12 g fat, 6 mg chol, 424 mg sodium, 53 g carbo, 4 g fiber, 13 g pro.

Fresh Herb Pasta Primavera

PREP 25 minutes **BAKE** 20 minutes

 8 ounces dried penne pasta or mostaccioli
   Parmesan Cream Sauce (recipe follows)
 ½ cup chopped red sweet pepper
 ⅓ cup sliced green onions
 ¼ cup dry sherry or chicken broth
 1 teaspoon olive oil
2½ to 3 cups assorted vegetables (such as shelled English peas, sugar snap peas, 2-inch asparagus tips, green beans, chopped zucchini and sliced baby carrots)
 1 cup lightly packed mixed fresh herbs (such as oregano, lemon thyme, summer savory and Italian (flat-leaf) parsley, snipped)
 ¼ teaspoon ground cumin
 1 cup halved cherry tomatoes
   Fresh herb sprigs (optional)

1. In a 4- or 4½-quart Dutch oven, cook pasta in 2 to 3 quarts lightly salted, boiling water until the pasta is tender but still firm. Drain well.

2. Prepare the Parmesan Cream Sauce. Return pasta to the Dutch oven, and stir in Parmesan Cream Sauce.

3. In a large skillet, cook sweet pepper and green onions in sherry and olive oil, uncovered, 3 to 4 minutes or until tender.

4. Add vegetables, herbs and cumin to the skillet. Cook, uncovered, for 2 minutes or until tender, stirring frequently.

5. Gently stir vegetables and cherry tomatoes into the pasta mixture in Dutch oven. Toss until just combined. Spread in an ungreased 13x9x2-inch (3-quart rectangular) baking dish.

6. Bake, uncovered, in a 375° oven about 20 minutes or until heated through. Garnish each serving with an herb sprig, if you like. **Makes 6 servings.**

Parmesan Cream Sauce: In a medium saucepan, melt ½ cup butter over medium heat. Stir in 3 tablespoons all-purpose flour. Cook and stir 2 minutes. Add 2 cups low-fat milk. Cook and stir until thickened and bubbly. Cook and stir 1 minute more. Remove from heat. Stir in ¾ cup grated Parmesan or Asiago cheese and freshly ground pepper to taste.

Per serving: 380 cal, 15 g fat, 40 mg chol, 284 mg sodium, 44 g carbo, 4 g fiber

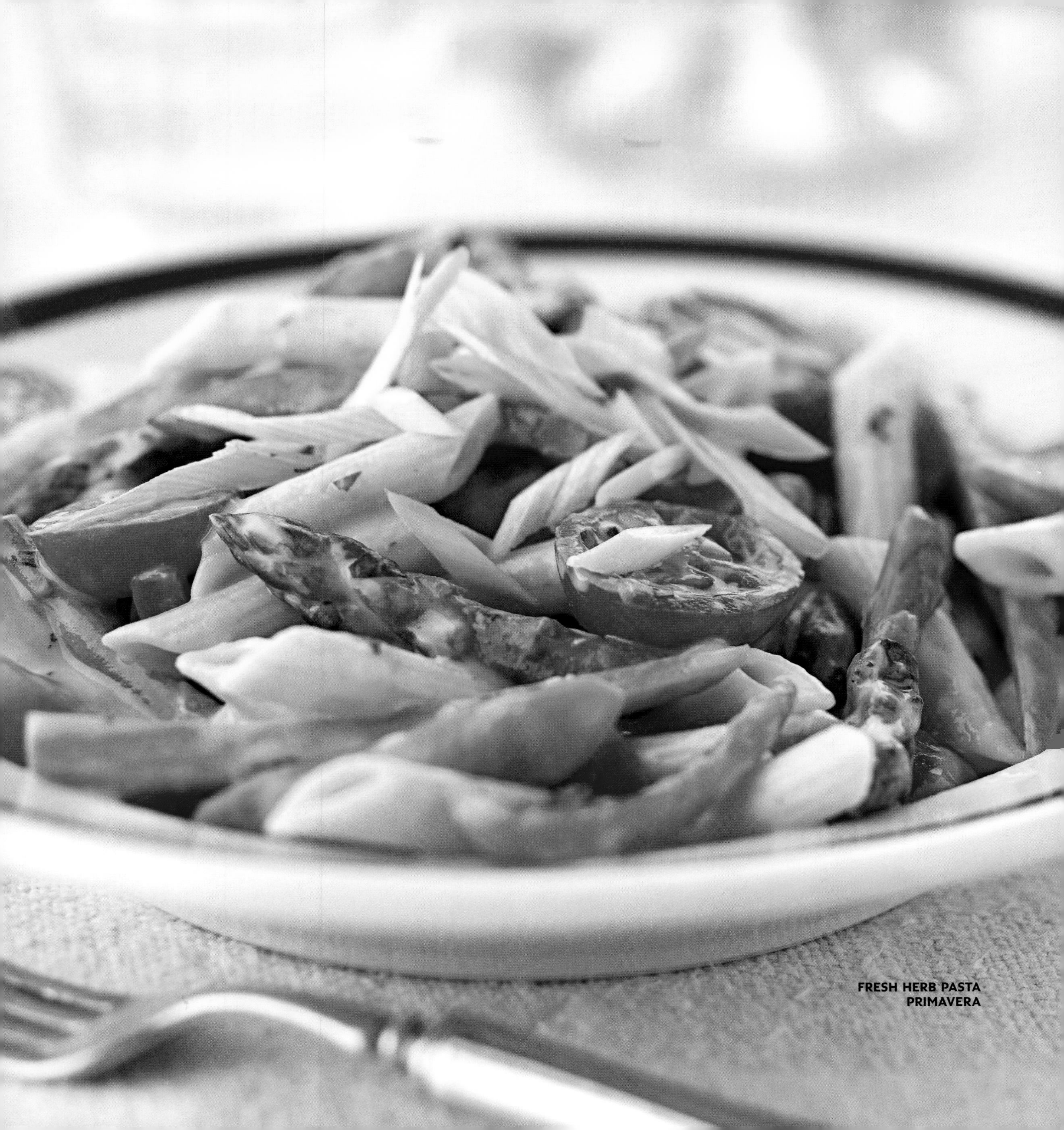

FRESH HERB PASTA PRIMAVERA

SWEET CORN PIZZA

Sweet Corn Pizza

PREP 25 minutes **BAKE** 12 minutes

Nonstick cooking spray
4 8-inch Italian bread shells (Boboli) or four
6- to 7-inch pita bread rounds
½ cup dried tomato pesto or basil pesto
1 14-ounce can artichoke hearts, drained
and coarsely chopped
1 cup fresh corn kernels
½ cup chopped green sweet pepper
8 ounces fresh mozzarella cheese, cut into
bite-size pieces; one 8-ounce package
shredded Italian blend cheeses (2 cups);
or 8 ounces semisoft goat cheese (chévre)
or feta, crumbled
Fresh basil leaves

1. Line a very large baking sheet (or two large baking sheets) with foil. Lightly coat foil with nonstick cooking spray. Place bread shells on prepared baking sheet. Bake in a 425° oven for 5 minutes. Remove bread shells from oven.

2. Spread tomato pesto over bread shell, leaving a ½-inch border. Arrange artichoke hearts, corn and sweet pepper on bread shell. Sprinkle with cheese. Bake for 12 to 15 minutes or until cheese is melted and pizzas are heated through. Sprinkle basil leaves over the tops of pizzas before serving. **Makes 4 to 8 servings.**

Per serving: 776 cal, 38 g fat, 43 mg chol, 1,455 mg sodium, 85 g carbo, 8 g fiber, 27 g pro.

Suncrest Gardens Farm's Garden Delight

Suncrest Gardens Farm in western Wisconsin is a working farm that also happens to make and sell pizzas cooked in a wood-fired oven and topped with local ingredients. Ever-abundant zucchini and summer squash top this vegetarian pizza. (Recipe pictured on page 52.)

PREP 3O minutes **BAKE** 15 minutes **COOL** 5 minutes

1 large onion, coarsely chopped
1 tablespoon olive oil
¼ teaspoon salt
1 13- to 15-inch Whole Wheat Pizza Dough
(see page 78) or desired pizza crust
1 8-ounce can tomato sauce or pizza sauce
1 large clove garlic, minced
2 cups shredded mozzarella cheese
(8 ounces)
½ cup lightly packed, finely shredded yellow
summer squash
½ cup lightly packed, finely shredded
zucchini
½ cup lightly packed, finely shredded carrot
2 medium fresh garden heirloom tomatoes
or desired red or yellow tomatoes, cored
and cut into ¼-inch-thick slices, or 1 cup
mixed baby tomatoes, halved
1 tablespoon snipped fresh basil

1. In a shallow baking pan, toss together the onion, olive oil and salt. Roast, uncovered, in a 450° oven for 20 minutes or until tender and golden brown, stirring occasionally. Remove from oven; set aside.

2. Bake Whole Wheat Pizza Dough crust in a 450° oven for 7 to 9 minutes or until crust is light brown. Remove from oven. (Or grill as directed in Whole Wheat Pizza Dough recipe.)

3. Spread tomato sauce evenly over crust; sprinkle with garlic. Sprinkle with cheese. Top with roasted onion, yellow squash, zucchini and carrot. Arrange tomato slices on top of the layer of vegetables. Sprinkle with the snipped basil.

4. Return to oven; bake for 8 to 10 minutes more or until heated through and bottom of crust is crisp and brown. (Or grill as directed.) Remove from oven; cool in pan on wire rack 5 minutes. **Makes one 13- to 15-inch pizza (four 2-wedge servings).**

Per serving: 449 cal, 21 g fat, 48 mg chol, 993 mg sodium, 48 g carbo, 6 g fiber, 22 g pro.

Suncrest Gardens Farm's Pesto Pizza

This tomatoey pizza from Suncrest Gardens Farm in western Wisconsin features kale pesto. Freeze homemade pesto in ice cube trays for use throughout the year. Once frozen, pop the cubes out of the tray into a freezer bag and pull them out as needed.

PREP 45 minutes **BAKE** 15 minutes **COOL** 5 minutes

1 12- to 14-inch Whole Wheat Pizza Dough (see page 78) or desired pizza crust
⅓ cup Kale Pesto (recipe follows) or purchased basil pesto*
1 cup shredded mozzarella cheese (4 ounces)
2 medium fresh garden heirloom tomatoes, or desired red or yellow tomatoes, cored and cut into ¼-inch-thick slices, or 1 cup mixed baby tomatoes, halved
½ to 1 teaspoon pizza seasoning

1. Bake whole wheat crust in 450° oven for 7 to 9 minutes or until light brown; remove from oven. (Or grill as directed in crust recipe.)

2. Prepare Kale Pesto. Spread Kale Pesto evenly over crust. Sprinkle with cheese. Arrange tomato slices over cheese. Sprinkle with pizza seasoning.

3. Bake about 8 to 10 minutes more or until heated through and crust bottom is crisp and brown. (Or grill as directed.) Remove from oven. Cool in pan on a wire rack for 5 minutes. Cut into wedges to serve. **Makes one 13- to 15-inch pizza (four 2-wedge servings).**

*Note: If you like, substitute 2 cups firmly packed fresh basil leaves, torn fresh arugula or spinach leaves with stems removed for the kale.

Per serving: 398 cal, 22 g fat, 34 mg chol, 434 mg sodium, 39 g carbo, 4 g fiber, 15 g pro.

Kale Pesto: Remove the leaves and stems from 1 pound of fresh kale. In a Dutch oven, bring 8 cups water to boiling. Drop leaves into water and cook, uncovered, for 3 to 5 minutes or until tender. Rinse leaves under cold running water; drain well. Wrap leaves in several layers of paper towel or a clean kitchen towel and squeeze out excess moisture. Coarsely chop and measure 2 cups. In a food processor or blender, combine the 2 cups chopped kale; ½ cup grated Parmesan or Romano cheese; ½ cup coarsely chopped walnuts; 2 large cloves garlic, quartered; and ½ teaspoon salt. With the machine running slowly, gradually add ¾ cup olive oil and process or blend to the consistency of soft butter. If you're not serving the pesto immediately, divide it into five ⅓-cup portions. Place each portion in a small airtight container and store in the refrigerator for up to 2 days or freeze for up to 3 months. Makes 1¾ cups.

Pizza is always a welcome meal. When the ingredients—juicy ripe tomatoes, greens, nutrient-rich vegetables and fresh herbs—ripen in the garden, the preparations can be simple. Great ingredients need little embellishment.

In high summer, the gardens of the Seed Savers Exchange in Decorah, Iowa, are awash in color. The exchange preserves and shares seeds for heirloom plant varieties. The gardens are as much about roots as they are about fruits and flowers. Visitors are welcome to visit for free from March through December.

Heirloom Tomato and Onion Quiche

Served with a mixed-green salad, this gorgeous quiche is just right for brunch or a light dinner.

PREP 25 minutes **BAKE** 35 minutes **STAND** 10 minutes

½ of a 15-ounce package (1 crust) rolled refrigerated unbaked piecrust
12 ounces assorted garden heirloom tomatoes or regular tomatoes, cut into ¼-inch-thick slices
1 tablespoon butter
½ cup chopped onion (1 medium)
3 eggs
¾ cup half-and-half, light cream or milk
3 tablespoons all-purpose flour
1 tablespoon snipped fresh basil or 1 teaspoon dried basil, crushed
½ teaspoon salt
¼ teaspoon dry mustard
⅛ teaspoon ground black pepper
1 cup shredded Swiss, cheddar, Monterey Jack and/or Havarti cheese (4 ounces)
Paprika

1. Let piecrust stand at room temperature according to package directions. Unroll piecrust into a 9-inch pie plate. Crimp edge as desired. Line unpricked pastry with a double thickness of foil. Bake in a 425° oven for 8 minutes. Remove foil. Bake for 4 to 5 minutes more or until pastry is set and dry. Remove from oven. Reduce oven temperature to 375°.

2. Meanwhile, place tomato slices on paper towels to absorb excess moisture. In a small skillet, melt butter over medium heat. Add onion. Cook until onion is tender but not brown, stirring occasionally.

3. In a medium bowl, whisk together eggs, half-and-half, flour, basil, salt, dry mustard and black pepper.

4. To assemble, sprinkle cheese onto bottom of the hot baked pastry shell. Spoon onion mixture over cheese. Arrange a single layer of tomato slices over cheese, overlapping slightly. Slowly pour egg mixture over tomatoes. Sprinkle paprika over egg mixture.

5. Bake, uncovered, for 35 to 40 minutes or until egg mixture is set in center. If necessary, cover edge of pie with foil for the last 5 to 10 minutes of baking to prevent overbrowning. Let stand 10 minutes before serving. **Makes 6 servings.**

Per serving: 352 cal, 23 g fat, 146 mg chol, 426 mg sodium, 26 g carbo, 1 g fiber, 11 g pro.

GRILLED GREEN
TOMATOES WITH
GARDEN HERB
SALAD

Grilled Green Tomatoes with Garden Herb Salad

This recipe is perfect just before the beginning of tomato season and just as it ends. Grilling the tomatoes imparts them with a smokiness that complements their natural tanginess. The earthiness of the herbs combined with the nuts and a little bit of sweetness from the golden raisins finishes off the dish with great balance.

PREP 40 minutes   **GRILL** 6 minutes

¾ cup loosely packed fresh Italian (flat-leaf) parsley leaves
¾ cup loosely packed fresh cilantro leaves
½ cup cut-up fresh chives
1 clove garlic, minced
½ cup olive oil
3 large green tomatoes
   Coarse (kosher) salt and ground black pepper
4 leaves iceberg lettuce, cut into thin bite-size strips (julienne)
¼ cup hazelnuts (filberts), toasted and coarsely chopped
¼ cup slivered almonds, toasted and coarsely chopped
¼ cup pistachios, toasted and coarsely chopped
¼ cup golden raisins
   Coarse (kosher) salt and ground black pepper
2 tablespoons sherry or white balsamic vinegar

1. On a cutting board, toss together parsley, cilantro and chives. Coarsely chop all the herbs together. In a medium bowl, combine herb mixture and garlic. Stir in olive oil; set aside.

2. Slice tomatoes into ½-inch slices. Generously season with salt and black pepper. For a charcoal grill: Grill tomato slices on rack of an uncovered grill directly over medium coals for 6 to 8 minutes or until tomatoes are tender, turning once halfway through grilling. (For a gas grill: Preheat grill. Reduce heat to medium. Place tomato slices on grill rack over heat. Cover; grill as above.)

3. Transfer tomatoes to a platter, arranging slices in a single layer. Spoon some of the herb oil over tomatoes; turn slices over and spoon on remaining herb oil.

4. In a separate bowl, combine the lettuce, hazelnuts, almonds, pistachios and raisins. Season to taste with salt and pepper. Drizzle vinegar over salad; toss lightly to coat evenly.

5. Spoon salad atop tomatoes. **Makes 4 servings.**

Per serving: 445 cal, 40 g fat, 0 mg chol, 182 mg sodium, 20 g carbo, 5 g fiber, 7 g pro.

Watermelon, Feta and Mint Salad

Fans of sweet-salty flavors will love this simple five-ingredient salad that combines sweet melon with tangy, salty feta cheese.

PREP 15 minutes   **CHILL** 2 hours

4 cups 1- to 2-inch chunks seedless red and/or yellow watermelon
4 ounces feta cheese, coarsely crumbled
¼ cup loosely packed mint leaves, torn into rough pieces
2 tablespoons extra virgin olive oil
   Freshly ground black pepper

In a large bowl, combine watermelon, feta cheese, mint and oil. Season to taste with black pepper. Cover and chill for 2 to 4 hours to blend flavors. Serve with grilled pork, chicken or fish. **Makes 6 servings.**

Per serving: 120 cal, 9 g fat, 17 mg chol, 210 mg sodium, 9 g carbo, 0 g fiber, 3 g pro.

Old-Fashioned Scalloped Corn

PREP 25 minutes **BAKE** 35 minutes **STAND** 10 minutes

3 tablespoons butter or margarine

¾ cup coarsely crushed saltine crackers (about 10 crackers)

1 large onion, finely chopped (1 cup)

2 cups fresh corn kernels or one 10-ounce package frozen whole kernel corn, thawed

1 14.75-ounce can cream-style corn

1 cup coarsely crushed saltine crackers (about 14 to 15 crackers)

1 cup milk, half-and-half or light cream

1 4-ounce jar diced pimiento, drained

3 eggs, lightly beaten

½ teaspoon ground black pepper or ¼ teaspoon cayenne pepper

¼ teaspoon paprika (optional)

½ cup shredded Swiss, Gruyére, cheddar or provolone cheese (2 ounces) (optional)

1. Grease a 2-quart oval baking dish, 2-quart round casserole dish or 8x8x2-inch square baking dish (2-quart); set aside.

2. For topping: In a 12-inch skillet, melt 2 tablespoons of the butter over medium heat. Add the ¾ cup crushed crackers. Cook and stir until crackers are light brown; remove from skillet and set aside.

3. In the same skillet, melt the remaining 1 tablespoon butter over medium heat. Add onion. Cook onion until tender, stirring occasionally. Stir in corn, cream-style corn, the 1 cup crushed crackers, milk, drained pimiento, eggs, black pepper and, if you like, paprika.

4. Transfer corn mixture to the prepared baking dish. Sprinkle on topping.

5. Bake, uncovered, in a 325° oven for 35 to 40 minutes or until center is set and a knife inserted near center comes out clean. Remove from oven. If you like, sprinkle with cheese. Let stand for 10 minutes before serving. **Makes 8 servings.**

Old-Fashioned Scalloped Corn with Ham: Prepare as directed above. Cut 6 ounces cooked boneless ham into bite-size cubes. Stir into corn mixture in skillet.

Per serving: 204 cal, 8 g fat, 93 mg chol, 327 mg sodium, 29 g carbo, 2 g fiber, 7 g pro.

Along Midwest backroads, farm stands offer a serendipitous taste of season and place. Enjoy an ice cream on-site or purchase at-peak produce to enjoy at home.

Cornmeal Griddle Cakes with Sauteed Corn

These bacon-flavored griddle cakes make a delicious side dish to grilled chicken or fish or—served with fresh fruit or a simple salad—a light supper.

PREP 30 minutes **STAND** 5 minutes **COOK** 4 minutes per batch

4 ears of fresh corn or one 10-ounce package frozen whole kernel corn, thawed (2 cups)
4 slices bacon
1 medium onion, chopped (½ cup)
1 cup buttermilk or sour milk*
1 egg, lightly beaten
1 tablespoon snipped fresh chives
¾ cup all-purpose flour
½ cup blue or yellow cornmeal
1 tablespoon sugar
1½ teaspoons baking powder
¼ teaspoon baking soda
¼ teaspoon salt
Crème fraîche or dairy sour cream
Snipped fresh chives (optional)

1. Remove and discard husks. Use a vegetable brush to remove silks; rinse corn. Holding the ear at an angle, use a sharp knife to cut down across the tips of the kernels at two-thirds depth; do not scrape. Measure 2 cups fresh corn kernels.

2. In a very large skillet, cook bacon until crisp. Remove bacon from skillet; reserving drippings in skillet. Drain bacon on paper towels and crumble finely; set aside.

3. Cook corn and onion in the reserved drippings over medium heat about 5 minutes or until tender. Cool slightly. Place half of the corn mixture (about ¾ cup) in a food processor or blender. Cover and process or blend until nearly smooth. Transfer to a medium bowl. Stir in buttermilk, egg and the 1 tablespoon chives.

4. In a large bowl, stir together flour, cornmeal, sugar, baking powder, baking soda and salt. Add buttermilk mixture all at once to flour mixture. Stir just until moistened (batter should be slightly lumpy). Stir in the remaining corn mixture and bacon. Let batter stand for 5 minutes.

5. Heat a lightly greased griddle or heavy large skillet over medium heat until a few drops of water dance across the surface. For each griddle cake, spoon about ¼ cup batter into skillet. Spread batter, if necessary, into a 3-inch circle in diameter. Cook about 2 minutes on each side, turning when griddle cakes are golden brown and edges are slightly dry.

6. Serve warm with crème fraîche. If you like, sprinkle with additional chives. **Makes 6 servings.**

*Note: To make 1 cup sour milk, place 1 tablespoon lemon juice or vinegar in a glass measure cup. Add enough milk to equal 1 cup total liquid; stir. Let stand for 5 minutes before using.

Per serving: 389 cal, 22 g fat, 81 mg chol, 492 mg sodium, 39 g carbo, 2 g fiber, 10 g pro.

Corn on the Cob with Flavored Butters

Cook sweet corn 3 to 5 minutes in boiling water, then try a new taste with one of these flavored butters. They're great on other veggies, too!

Serrano Chile Butter: In a mixing bowl, beat ½ cup butter, softened; 2 tablespoons grated Parmesan cheese; ½ to 1 fresh serrano or jalapeño chile pepper, seeded and finely chopped (see Note, page 58); 1½ teaspoons lime juice; and ¼ teaspoon chili powder with electric mixer until well combined. Cover; chill 1 to 24 hours. Bring to room temperature before serving. Makes ⅔ cup.

Gorgonzola-Bacon Butter: In a mixing bowl, beat ½ cup butter, softened; 1 tablespoon finely crumbled crisp-cooked bacon; and 1 to 2 tablespoons crumbled Gorgonzola or blue cheese with electric mixer until well combined. Cover; chill 1 to 24 hours. Bring to room temperature before serving. Makes ½ cup.

Lemon-Parsley Butter: In a mixing bowl, beat ½ cup butter, softened; 1 tablespoon finely snipped fresh Italian (flat-leaf) parsley; ½ teaspoon finely shredded lemon peel; 1½ teaspoons lemon juice; and ¼ teaspoon sugar with electric mixer until well combined. Cover; chill 1 to 24 hours. Bring butter to room temperature before serving. Makes about ½ cup.

How do you eat your corn on the cob? In neat, methodical rows? In circles around the cob? In completely random bites? Whatever tack is taken, the end result is the same: Smiles all around.

Heirloom tomatoes come in a rainbow of colors and a delightful variety of sizes and shapes. All they really need is slicing and a sprinkle of sea salt.

Grilled Tomato Melts

PREP 15 minutes **BAKE** 15 minutes

  3 large tomatoes (about 8 ounces each) or a
     variety of smaller tomatoes (about
     1½ pounds total)
  4 ounces Monterey Jack cheese with
     jalapeño peppers or Monterey Jack
     cheese, shredded (1½ cups)
  1 small green, yellow, purple or red sweet
     pepper, finely chopped (about ½ cup)
  ¼ cup toasted sliced almonds

1. Cut each tomato into four slices, about ½ inch thick. If using smaller tomatoes, halve each one. For each of four servings, arrange three tomato slices, overlapping slightly, in a foil-lined 15x10x1-inch baking pan. (Or if using smaller tomatoes, arrange in a single layer in a foil-lined 15x10x1-inch baking pan.) Sprinkle with shredded cheese, finely chopped pepper and toasted almonds. Bake in a 350° oven about 15 minutes or until cheese is bubbly. Carefully lift with a large metal spatula to individual plates, allowing excess juices to drain off.

2. To prepare on a grill, arrange ingredients as above in a shallow disposable foil pan. In a grill with a cover, arrange medium-hot coals around the edge of the grill; test for medium heat above the center of the grill. Place the pan with the tomatoes in the center of the grill rack. Grill, covered, for 12 to 15 minutes or until cheese is bubbly. **Makes 4 servings.**

Make-ahead tip: Arrange tomato slices in baking pan and sprinkle with cheese, pepper and nuts. Cover and chill up to 4 hours. Bake or grill as above.

Per serving: 203 cal, 14 g fat, 25 mg chol, 172 mg sodium, 13 g carbo, 2 g fiber, 10 g pro.

Grilled Zucchini with Tomatoes

PREP 15 minutes **GRILL** 19 minutes **STAND** 5 minutes

  2 medium zucchini
  4 large roma tomatoes
    Olive oil
  2 large red or green sweet peppers,
     quartered and seeded*
  ½ cup balsamic vinegar
  2 tablespoons orange juice
  1 tablespoon honey
  8 fresh basil leaves, snipped
     (about 1 tablespoon)
    Dash dried oregano, crushed

1. Bias-cut zucchini into ½-inch slices. Cut tomatoes into ½-inch slices. Brush these vegetables on all sides with olive oil.

2. Grill zucchini and tomato slices on the rack of an uncovered grill directly over medium coals for 4 to 6 minutes, turning once. Remove from grill. Grill sweet peppers about 15 minutes or until skins are blistered and browned. Transfer peppers to a brown paper bag; close bag and set aside for 5 to 10 minutes. Peel off skins. Cover and chill vegetables for at least 30 minutes.

3. For dressing, in a small bowl, combine vinegar, orange juice and honey. Whisk or beat with a fork until well blended. Stir in basil and oregano. Drizzle some of the dressing over chilled vegetables. Store remaining dressing in the refrigerator for up to 2 weeks. **Makes 6 to 8 servings.**

*Note: If you like, substitute canned roasted red sweet peppers for the grilled fresh peppers. You'll find them in Italian food stores and most large supermarkets.

Per serving: 78 cal, 3 g fat, 0 mg chol, 10 mg sodium, 14 g carbo, 2 g fiber, 1 g pro.

North Dakota Juneberry Pie

Called the Blueberry of the Northern Plains, juneberries (also known as serviceberries) give bakers in North Dakota and South Dakota a reason to warm kitchens in summer. Pies featuring the berry bake to a deep purply red. Every forkful has a nutty almond flavor.

PREP 35 minutes **BAKE** 55 minutes

Pastry for a Single-Crust Pie* (recipe follows)
½ cup sugar
¼ cup all-purpose flour
2 cups fresh juneberries or fresh or frozen blueberries
2 cups halved fresh strawberries or fresh or frozen blueberries
1 cup fresh or frozen red raspberries or blackberries
2 teaspoons finely shredded lemon peel
½ cup all-purpose flour
⅓ cup sugar
3 tablespoons butter
⅓ cup sliced almonds, coarsely chopped

1. Prepare Pastry for a Single-Crust Pie. On a lightly floured surface, use your hands to slightly flatten dough. Roll dough from center to edge into a 12-inch circle. Wrap pastry circle around a rolling pin; unroll into a 9-inch pie plate. Ease pastry into pie plate without stretching it. Trim pastry to ½ inch beyond edge of pie plate. Fold under extra pastry even with edge of plate. Crimp edge as desired. Do not prick pastry.

2. For filling: In a large bowl, stir together the ½ cup sugar and the ¼ cup flour. Add berries and lemon peel; toss gently to coat. (If using frozen berries, let mixture stand about 45 minutes or until berries are partially thawed but still icy.) Transfer mixture to the pastry-lined pie plate.

3. For crumb topping: In a medium bowl, stir together the ½ cup flour and the ⅓ cup sugar. Using a pastry blender, cut in butter until mixture resembles coarse crumbs. Stir in almonds. Sprinkle evenly over filling.

4. To prevent overbrowning, cover edge of pie with foil. Bake in a 375° oven for 25 minutes (or 50 minutes for frozen berries). Remove foil. Bake for 30 to 35 minutes more or until filling is bubbly and topping is golden brown. Cool on a wire rack. **Makes 8 servings.**

Pastry for a Single-Crust Pie: In a medium bowl, stir together 1½ cups all-purpose flour and ½ teaspoon salt. Using a pastry blender, cut in ¼ cup shortening and ¼ cup cut-up butter, until pieces are pea size. Sprinkle 1 tablespoon ice water over part of the flour mixture; gently toss with a fork. Push moistened pastry to the side of the bowl. Repeat moistening flour mixture, using 1 tablespoon ice water at a time, until all of the flour mixture is moistened (¼ to ⅓ cup ice water total). Gather flour mixture into a ball, kneading gently until it holds together.

*Note: To save time, use half of a 15-ounce package (one crust) rolled refrigerated unbaked piecrust instead of the homemade pastry. Let stand according to package directions before easing into pie plate.

Per serving: 416 cal, 19 g fat, 27 mg chol, 219 mg sodium, 59 g carbo, 4 g fiber, 5 g pro.

FINNISH
BLUEBERRY PIE

Finnish Blueberry Pie (Mustikkapiirakka)

PREP 25 minutes   **CHILL** 1 hour   **BAKE** 50 minutes   **STAND** 30 minutes

½ cup butter, softened
1 egg
¼ cup half-and-half or light cream
1¼ cups all-purpose flour
4 cups fresh blueberries
¼ cup granulated sugar
1 tablespoon fine dry bread crumbs
  Powdered sugar (optional)
  Whipped cream (optional)

1. In a medium mixing bowl, beat butter with an electric mixer on medium to high speed for 30 seconds. Add the egg. Beat until combined, scraping sides of bowl occasionally. Beat in half-and-half. Stir in flour until well-combined. Remove dough from bowl; gently shape into a ball. Flatten dough into a 6-inch disc. Cover dough with plastic wrap and chill for 1 hour or until dough is easy to handle. On a lightly floured surface, roll pastry to a 13-inch circle. To transfer pastry, wrap it around the rolling pin; unroll onto a large baking sheet.

2. In a large bowl, combine blueberries, granulated sugar and bread crumbs. Gently toss until coated. Carefully mound blueberry mixture in center of crust, leaving a 2-inch border. Carefully fold the pastry border up and over blueberries, pleating the pastry as necessary to fit.

3. Bake in a 325° oven about 50 minutes or until crust is golden and filling is bubbly. Cool for 30 minutes on the baking sheet. Transfer pie to serving platter; cool completely before serving. If you like, dust edges with powdered sugar and serve with whipped cream. **Makes 8 servings.**

Per serving: 254 cal, 13 g fat, 60 mg chol, 117 mg sodium, 31 g carbo, 2 g fiber, 4 g pro.

Uncovered Blueberry Pie

Looking for a fast dessert that showcases a summer fruit? This one-crust, no-bake blueberry pie can be ready for the table in less than an hour. Or make it ahead of time and served it chilled.

PREP 15 minutes   **COOK** 10 minutes

¾ cup sugar
3 tablespoons cornstarch
⅛ teaspoon salt
1 cup water
3 cups fresh blueberries
1 tablespoon butter
1 9-inch baked pie shell
  Sweetened whipped cream

In a medium saucepan, combine sugar, cornstarch and salt. Stir in the water and 1 cup of the blueberries. Cook and stir over medium heat until thickened. Remove from heat. Stir in remaining 2 cups blueberries and butter until butter is melted. Cool completely. Pour into pie shell. If desired, cover and chill in refrigerator until ready to serve. Serve with whipped cream. **Makes 8 servings.**

Per serving: 261 cal, 10 g fat, 4 mg chol, 122 mg sodium, 40 g carbo, 3 g fiber, 2 g pro.

What better time to make pie than July and August, when Michigan blueberries are ripe and ready for plucking?

Raspberry Pie

PREP 25 minutes **BAKE** 45 minutes

- 4 cups fresh or frozen raspberries
- 1 cup sugar
- 3 tablespoons quick-cooking tapioca
- 2 tablespoons butter, melted
- 1 15-ounce package refrigerated unbaked piecrusts (2 crusts)
- Vanilla ice cream (optional)

1. For filling: In a large bowl, combine raspberries, sugar, tapioca and butter. Toss until combined. (If using frozen raspberries, let the mixture stand for 15 to 30 minutes or until the fruit is partially thawed but still icy. Stir well.)

2. For bottom crust, unwrap refrigerated pastry according to package directions. Fit one unbaked crust into a 9-inch pie plate. Trim pastry to ½ inch beyond edge of pie plate.

3. For lattice top, roll remaining unbaked crust to a 12-inch circle. Cut pastry into ½-inch-wide strips.

4. Spoon the raspberry mixture into the pastry-lined pie plate.

5. Weave strips over the filling to make a lattice. Press the ends of the strips into the rim of the crust. Fold bottom pastry over strips; seal and crimp edge. Cover edge with foil.

6. Place pie on a baking sheet. Bake in a 375° oven for 25 minutes. Remove foil. Bake for 20 to 25 minutes more or until the top is golden. (Or for frozen raspberries: Bake for 50 minutes. Remove foil; bake for 20 to 30 minutes more or until top is golden.) Cool the pie on a wire rack. Serve with ice cream, if you like. **Makes 6 to 8 servings.**

Per serving: 405 cal, 17 g fat, 18 mg chol, 231 mg sodium, 61 g carbo, 4 g fiber, 2 g pro.

Peach-Brown Butter Tart

A crusty sugar-almond streusel tops this custardy peach pie.

PREP 40 minutes **BAKE** 50 minutes

- ⅓ cup all-purpose flour
- ⅓ cup quick-cooking or regular rolled oats
- ¼ cup sliced almonds, toasted
- ¼ cup cold butter
- 2 tablespoons granulated sugar
- 2 tablespoons brown sugar
- 1½ teaspoons ground cinnamon
- ¾ teaspoon ground nutmeg
- ¼ teaspoon salt
- ¾ cup butter
- 3 eggs
- 1 cup granulated sugar
- ⅓ cup all-purpose flour
- 2 teaspoons vanilla
- ¼ teaspoon salt
- 2 cups sliced, peeled, fresh or frozen peaches
- ½ cup sliced almonds, toasted
- 1 teaspoon finely shredded lemon peel
- ¼ teaspoon ground nutmeg
- Baked Pastry Shell (recipe follows)

1. For streusel topping: In a food processor bowl, combine the ⅓ cup flour, the rolled oats, ¼ cup sliced almonds, ¼ cup butter, 2 tablespoons granulated sugar, 2 tablespoons brown sugar, the cinnamon, ¾ teaspoon nutmeg and ¼ teaspoon salt. Process until mixture is evenly crumbly. (Or chop almonds. In a medium bowl, combine almonds, flour, oats, granulated and brown sugars, cinnamon, nutmeg and salt. Using a pastry blender, cut in ¼ cup butter until the mixture is crumbly.) Set aside.

2. For filling: In a small saucepan, heat the ¾ cup butter over low heat until browned. Remove from heat. In a medium bowl, whisk together eggs, the 1 cup granulated sugar, ⅓ cup flour, the vanilla and ¼ teaspoon salt. Whisk in browned butter. Set aside.

3. In a large bowl, toss peaches with the ½ cup almonds, the lemon peel and the ¼ teaspoon nutmeg. Spoon mixture into Baked Pastry Shell. Pour the filling over peaches. Spoon streusel topping evenly over filling. Cover edge of pastry with foil.

4. Place pie plate on a baking sheet. Bake in a 350° oven for 50 to 55 minutes or until golden and set. Cool on a wire rack. Cover and chill in refrigerator to store. **Makes 8 servings.**

Baked Pastry Shell: In a large bowl, stir together 1¼ cups flour and ¼ teaspoon salt. Using a pastry blender, cut in ⅓ cup shortening until pieces are pea-size. Sprinkle 1 tablespoon cold water over part of the mixture; gently toss with a fork. Push moistened dough to the side of the bowl. Repeat moistening dough, using 1 tablespoon cold water at a time, until all the dough is moistened (4 to 5 tablespoons water total). Form dough into a ball. On a lightly floured surface, use your hands to slightly flatten dough. Roll dough from center to edge into a 12-inch circle. To transfer pastry, wrap it around the rolling pin. Unroll pastry into a 9-inch pie plate. Ease pastry into pie plate, being careful not to stretch pastry. Trim pastry to ½ inch beyond edge of pie plate. Fold under extra pastry. Crimp edge as desired. Generously prick bottom and side of pastry in pie plate with a fork. Prick all around where bottom and sides meet. Line pastry with a double thickness of foil. Bake in a 450° oven for 8 minutes. Remove foil. Bake for 5 to 6 minutes more or until golden. Cool on a wire rack.

Per serving: 641 cal, 38 g fat, 131 mg chol, 450 mg sodium, 69 g carbo, 3 g fiber, 8 g pro.

PEACH-BROWN
BUTTER TART

KIWI SUMMER
LIMEADE PIE

Kiwi Summer Limeade Pie

Refreshing and creamy, this make-ahead pie combines a tropical mix of macadamia nuts and kiwifruit.

PREP 20 minutes **CHILL** 8 hours

- 6 tablespoons coarsely chopped macadamia nuts
- 1 9-inch baked pastry shell
- 1 6-ounce can frozen limeade concentrate, thawed
- 1 4-serving-size package vanilla instant pudding and pie filling mix
- 2 8-ounce packages cream cheese, softened
- ¾ cup powdered sugar
- 3 medium kiwifruit, peeled, halved lengthwise and sliced
- 1 6-ounce carton lime low-fat yogurt
- 1½ cups frozen whipped dessert topping, thawed

1. Sprinkle 2 tablespoons of the macadamia nuts in the bottom of the pastry shell.

2. In a small bowl, whisk together limeade concentrate and vanilla pudding mix.

3. In a medium mixing bowl, beat cream cheese with an electric mixer for 30 seconds. Beat in powdered sugar. Add limeade mixture and beat well. Transfer ¾ cup of the mixture to another medium bowl; set aside. Spoon remaining mixture into the pastry shell. Top with two of the kiwifruit.

4. Beat yogurt into the reserved ¾ cup cream cheese mixture until combined. Fold in whipped topping. Spoon over filling in pastry shell. Cover and chill 8 to 24 hours. Garnish with remaining kiwifruit and nuts. **Makes 8 servings.**

Per serving: 579 cal, 34 g fat, 66 mg chol, 502 mg sodium, 63 g carbo, 1 g fiber, 6 g pro.

Mixed Cherry Clafouti

A clafouti is a country-French dessert made by topping a layer of fresh fruit—most commonly cherries—with a batter then baking it. It's often served warm with cream or ice cream.

PREP 25 minutes **BAKE** 45 minutes **COOL** 10 minutes

- ½ teaspoon butter
- ¾ cup all-purpose flour
- ¼ cup granulated sugar
- 4 eggs, slightly beaten
- 2 tablespoons plain nonfat yogurt or dairy sour cream
- 1¼ cups milk
- ¼ cup honey
- 2 tablespoons crème de cassis, fruit-flavor liqueur (raspberry or orange) or 2 tablespoons orange juice
- 2 cups fresh or frozen* unsweetened pitted sweet cherries (Bing, Lambert or Rainier)
- 1 cup fresh or frozen* unsweetened pitted tart cherries (Morella or Montmorency)
  Vanilla frozen yogurt or mango sorbet
  Powdered sugar
  Fresh mint sprigs

1. Butter a 10- or 11-inch quiche dish or an 8x8x2-inch (2-quart square) baking dish. Set aside. In a medium bowl, combine flour and granulated sugar.

2. In another medium bowl, combine the eggs, yogurt, milk, and honey; whisk until mixture is nearly smooth. Stir in liqueur. Add egg mixture to flour mixture; whisk until mixture is nearly smooth (do not overwork).

3. Add one-third of the batter (1 cup) to the prepared dish. Place dish on the lower rack of a 350° oven. Bake about 10 minutes or until almost firm. Remove from oven and flatten, if necessary, to make room for cherry mixture.

4. In a large bowl, combine cherries and the remaining batter. Pour cherry mixture on top of baked batter. Return to oven. Bake for 35 to 40 minutes more or until golden brown and a knife inserted near the center comes out clean.

5. Cool in dish on a wire rack for 10 minutes. (The clafouti will fall as it cools.) To serve, cut into eight wedges or squares. Transfer warm clafouti to shallow dessert dishes. Place a scoop of yogurt next to each clafouti wedge or square. Sprinkle with powdered sugar. Garnish with a sprig of mint. **Makes 8 servings.**

*Note: Thaw and drain frozen cherries before using.

Per serving: 201 cal, 4 g fat, 111 mg chol, 60 mg sodium, 35 g carbo, 1 g fiber, 6 g pro.

PEACH KUCHEN

Peach Kuchen

German settlers brought the recipe for this tender coffee cake to the northern plains. The industrious pioneers changed the taste by folding local fruits into the batter: apple, gooseberry, plum and even no-fruit cottage cheese. Here's a biscuitlike version with summery peaches. Serve it warm for breakfast or with ice cream for dessert.

PREP 25 minutes **BAKE** 40 minutes **COOL** 20 minutes

1½ cups all-purpose flour
¾ cup granulated sugar
1½ teaspoons baking powder
¼ teaspoon salt
¼ teaspoon ground nutmeg or cinnamon
¼ cup butter
1 egg, lightly beaten
½ cup milk
2 cups sliced fresh peaches or frozen
    unsweetened peach slices, thawed and
    well drained on paper towels
⅓ cup packed brown sugar
1 tablespoon light-color corn syrup
1 tablespoon butter
1 teaspoon lemon juice
    Vanilla or peach ice cream

1. Grease and flour a 9x9x2-inch baking pan. Set aside.

2. In a medium bowl, mix flour, sugar, baking powder, salt and nutmeg. Using a pastry blender, cut in the ¼ cup butter until mixture resembles coarse crumbs. Make a well in center of flour mixture. In a small bowl, combine egg and milk. Add egg mixture all at once to flour mixture. Stir just until moistened (batter should be lumpy).

3. Spread batter into prepared pan. Halve any large peach slices. Arrange peach slices in a single layer on top of batter.

4. For topping: In a small saucepan, combine brown sugar, corn syrup, the 1 tablespoon butter and the lemon juice. Bring to boiling. Quickly drizzle over peach slices.

5. Bake in a 350° oven for 40 to 45 minutes or until a toothpick inserted in the center of cake comes out clean. Cool in pan on wire rack for 20 minutes. Serve warm with ice cream. **Makes 9 servings.**

Per serving: 410 cal, 15 g fat, 73 mg chol, 224 mg sodium, 63 g carbo, 2 g fiber, 6 g pro.

Blueberry Pound Cake

Make good use of farm-fresh blueberries with this simple fruit-filled pound cake. Because it makes 10 to 12 servings, this recipe is ideal for summer entertaining.

PREP 30 minutes **STAND** 30 minutes
BAKE 1 hour **COOL** 15 minutes

½ cup butter
3 eggs
3½ cups all-purpose flour
2 teaspoons baking powder
¼ teaspoon salt
2 cups sugar
4 cups fresh blueberries
1 cup milk

1. Allow butter and eggs to stand at room temperature for 30 minutes. Grease a 10-inch tube pan; set aside. In a large bowl, sift together the flour, baking powder and salt; set aside.

2. In a very large mixing bowl, beat the butter and sugar with an electric mixer on medium speed until mixture is well combined. Beat in eggs. Stir blueberries into flour mixture. By hand, stir blueberry mixture into butter mixture. Stir in milk just until combined. Spread batter in prepared pan.

3. Bake in a 325° oven for 60 to 75 minutes or until a wooden skewer inserted near center comes out clean. Cool on wire rack for 15 minutes. Loosen cake from edge of pan with a narrow metal spatula. Remove cake from pan; cool completely on wire rack. **Makes 10 to 12 servings.**

Per serving: 444 cal, 12 g fat, 91 mg chol, 209 mg sodium, 77 g carbo, 4 g fiber, 7 g pro.

Sweet Corn Ice Cream

PREP 1 hour 15 minutes   COOK 30 minutes   STAND 1 hour 20 minutes   CHILL 8 hours   FREEZE 4 hours

6 to 7 fresh ears of corn or 3 cups frozen
  whole kernel corn
2 cups half-and-half, light cream or whole
  milk
¾ cup sugar
6 inches stick cinnamon, broken into pieces
1 whole nutmeg, broken into pieces
8 egg yolks
2 tablespoons peach preserves
2 cups whipping cream
1 tablespoon lime juice
1 teaspoon kosher salt or ½ teaspoon salt
  Caramel-flavor ice cream topping
    (optional)
  Caramel corn or kettle corn (optional)

1. Remove and discard husks. Use a
vegetable brush to remove silks; rinse.
Place one ear of corn at a time in a shallow
pan. Holding the ear at an angle, use a
sharp knife to cut down across the tips of
the kernels at two-thirds depth. Using the
dull side of the knife; scrape the corn cob
to release the milky juices into the pan.
Measure 3 cups cut corn and juices. Break
the cobs in half.

2. In a food processor or blender, combine
1½ cups of the corn and 1 cup of the half-
and-half. Cover and process or blend until
nearly smooth. Transfer corn mixture to
a large heavy saucepan. Repeat with the
remaining 1½ cups corn and the 1 cup
half-and-half. Add cob pieces, ½ cup of the
sugar, the cinnamon and nutmeg to corn
mixture in saucepan. Cook over medium
heat, stirring frequently, just until tiny
bubbles form around the edge. Reduce heat
to low and cook, stirring frequently, for
15 minutes. Remove from heat; cover and
let stand for 1 hour. Using tongs, remove
corn cobs and cinnamon shaking off as
much of the cream mixture as possible.

3. Pour corn mixture through a fine-mesh
sieve into a large bowl, pressing on solids
with back of a spoon; discard solids.
Transfer the strained mixture to a clean
large heavy saucepan. Add egg yolks, the
remaining ¼ cup sugar and the peach
preserves; whisk until combined. Cook
and stir constantly over medium heat until
custard coats the back of a metal spoon.
Remove saucepan from heat and let stand
for 20 minutes.

4. Strain the custard through a fine-mesh
sieve into a large bowl placed in a larger
bowl of ice water. Stir custard until cooled.
Stir in whipping cream, lime juice and
salt. Cover the surface of the custard with
plastic wrap and chill in the refrigerator for
8 to 24 hours.

5. Spoon chilled custard into a 4- to 5-quart
ice cream freezer. Freeze according to
the manufacturer's directions. Ripen ice
cream at least 4 hours.* If you like, serve
with caramel topping and caramel or kettle
corn. **Makes 6 (1-cup) servings.**

*Note: To ripen ice cream in a traditional-
style ice cream freezer, after churning,
remove the lid and dasher and cover the
top of freezer can with waxed paper or foil.
Plug the hole in the lid with a small piece of
cloth; replace the lid. Pack the outer freezer
bucket with enough ice and rock salt to
cover the top of the freezer can, using
4 cups ice to 1 cup salt. When using an ice-
cream freezer with an insulated can, after
churning, remove dasher; replace lid. Cover
the lid with ice and cover with a towel.

Per serving: 321 cal, 23 g fat, 209 mg chol, 200 mg
sodium, 27 g carbo, 1 g fiber, 5 g pro.

CRISPY CHERRY-
ALMOND BARS WITH
MARSHMALLOWS

Easy Peach Ice Cream

PREP 15 minutes **FREEZE** according to manufacturer's directions

- 2 pounds fresh peaches or two 16-ounce packages frozen unsweetened peach slices, thawed
- 2 14-ounce cans sweetened condensed milk, chilled
- 1⅓ cups milk

Wash fresh peaches and remove the pits, if using. Cut up fresh peaches, if using. Place half of the fresh or thawed peaches in a blender. Cover and blend until smooth. Transfer pureed peaches to a large bowl. Repeat with remaining peaches. You should have about 2¾ cups pureed peaches. Add sweetened condensed milk and milk to pureed peaches; stir until well combined. Transfer the mixture to a 4- or 5-quart ice cream freezer. Freeze according to the manufacturer's directions. If you like, ripen for 4 hours before serving. **Makes 2O servings.**

Per serving: 151 cal, 4 g fat, 15 mg chol, 57 mg sodium, 26 g carbo, 1 g fiber, 4 g pro.

Tropical Berry Pops

PREP 25 minutes **FREEZE** About 6 hours

- 2 cups white grape juice, pineapple juice, guava nectar or apple juice
- 1 8-ounce can crushed pineapple (juice pack)
- ½ cup fresh blackberries, black or red raspberries, and/or blueberries
- ½ cup sliced fresh strawberries

1. In a blender, combine juice and undrained crushed pineapple. Cover and blend until smooth. Divide blackberries and strawberries among twelve 4- to 6-ounce paper cups or freezer pop molds. Pour blended mixture over the fruit. Cover each with foil.

2. Use the tip of a sharp knife to make a slit in the foil in each of the foil tops. For handles, insert a flat wooden crafts stick or plastic spoon into each cup through hole. (Or add sticks and cover pop molds.) Freeze about 6 hours or until firm. To serve, remove foil and tear off paper cups. Serve immediately. **Makes 12 (1 pop) servings.**

Per serving: 43 cal, O g fat, O mg chol, 5 mg sodium, 11 g carbo, 1 g fiber, O g pro.

Berry Super Smoothies: In a blender, mix a large ripe banana, one 6-ounce carton vanilla fat-free yogurt and ¾ cup fat-free milk. Remove foil, tear off paper cups and remove sticks from four of the Tropical Berry Pops. Add the pops to the blender. Cover and blend until the mixture is smooth. Pour mixture into three serving glasses. If you like, top each drink with a fresh mint sprig. Serve immediately. Makes 3 smoothies.

Crispy Cherry-Almond Bars with Marshmallows

PREP 2O minutes **COOL** 1 hour

- 3 tablespoons butter
- 1 1O-ounce package regular marshmallows
- ½ cup dried tart cherries, snipped, or raisins
- ½ cup toasted slivered almonds
- 3 cups crisp rice cereal
- 3 cups chocolate-flavor crisp rice cereal

1. In a large saucepan, melt butter over low heat. Add the marshmallows; stir and heat until melted. Stir in cherries and almonds. Fold in the cereals.

2. Turn mixture into a buttered 13x9x2-inch pan. Press evenly into pan using lightly buttered hands. Cool 1 hour. Cut into bars. **Makes 24 bars.**

Per bar: 98 cal, 3 g fat, 4 mg chol, 75 mg sodium, 19 g carbo, 1 g fiber, 1 g pro.

PUMPKIN-APPLE
BUTTER PIE, PAGE 172

Fall

APPETIZERS

Buffalo Chicken Wings with Blue Cheese Dressing 129

Gouda and Red Onion Pizza 133

Habanero Hot Wings 129

Jack Cheese and Smoky Chipotle Fondue 134

Slim Tex-Mex Taco Dip 133

Slow-Cooker Sweet-Hot Nuts 134

Toasted Ravioli 130

BREADS

Apple Scones with Spiced Maple Butter 121

Best Potato Rolls 125

Garlic and Rosemary Knots 125

Maple-Sweet Potato Sticky Buns 122

Orange-Glazed Sweet Potato Breakfast Braid 118

Pumpkin-Currant Scones 125

The BMC² 126

MAIN DISHES

Angel Chicken 156

Beef Short Ribs with Cranberry-Port Gravy 138

Cider-Brined Coho Salmon with Dijon Cream 160

Cincinnati-Style Chili 145

Harvest Chipotle Chili 149

Hearty Pork and Ale Stew 152

Italian Beef Sandwiches 142

Pasties 141

Pulled Pork Sandwiches with Root Beer Barbecue Sauce 150

Rigatoni with Spinach, Walnuts, Sweet Potatoes and Goat Cheese 162

Roasted Chicken Breasts with Caramelized Onions and Fall Fruit 152

Turkey Onion Soup 156

The Ultimate Chicken and Noodle Casserole 155

Ultimate Grilled Cheese and Ham Panini with Parsnip Fries 146

Venison Sausage Focaccia 159

Wagyu Beef Carbonnade 138

SIDES

Butternut Squash Risotto with Honeycrisp Apples 162

Calabaza Squash Gratin with Goat Cheese, Sage and Hazelnuts 168

Praline Sweet Potatoes 167

Shaved Vegetable Salad with Brown Butter Vinaigrette 164

Wheat Berry Waldorf Salad 167

SWEETS

Crumb-Topped Apple Trio Pie 171

Indulgent Caramel Apples 179

Pumpkin-Apple Butter Pie 172

Pumpkin-Praline Layer Cake 175

Spiced Pear-Cranberry Cobbler 176

Orange-Glazed Sweet Potato Breakfast Braid

Infused with a mellow blend of spices, citrus peel and raisins, this moist morning bread bakes up into a gorgeous sweet-potato gold.

PREP 50 minutes **RISE** 1 hour 40 minutes **REST** 10 minutes **BAKE** 25 minutes

¾ cup milk
7 tablespoons unsalted butter, softened
⅓ cup granulated sugar
4 to 4½ cups bread flour, divided
1 package active dry yeast
1 teaspoon salt
¼ teaspoon ground cinnamon
¼ teaspoon ground ginger
¼ teaspoon ground cardamom
2 eggs, lightly beaten
½ cup cooked, mashed and cooled sweet potato
1 tablespoon finely shredded orange peel
1 teaspoon finely shredded lemon peel
1 cup golden raisins
1½ cups powdered sugar
4 to 5 tablespoons orange juice

1. In a small saucepan, heat milk, 6 tablespoons of the butter and the granulated sugar over medium heat until butter is almost melted and an instant-read thermometer registers 110° to 115°.

2. Meanwhile, in a large mixing bowl, combine 2 cups of the flour, the yeast, salt, cinnamon, ginger and cardamom. Add the warm milk mixture, eggs, sweet potato, orange peel and lemon peel. Beat with an electric mixer for 4 minutes. Use a wooden spoon to stir in raisins and enough of the remaining flour to make a soft dough.

3. Turn dough out onto a lightly floured surface. Knead in enough of the remaining flour to make a moderately stiff dough that is smooth and elastic (6 to 8 minutes). Shape into a ball. Place in a lightly greased bowl, turning once to grease dough surface. Cover and let rise in a warm place until double in size (about 1 hour).

4. Punch dough down. Turn dough out onto a lightly floured surface. Divide in half. Cover; let rest 10 minutes. Divide one half into three equal portions. Shape each into a 10- to 12-inch rope. Place ropes, side by side, on a baking sheet lined with parchment paper. Braid ropes, starting from the center. Pinch ends to seal. Repeat with remaining dough. Brush loaves with some of the remaining 1 tablespoon butter. Cover and let rise in a warm place until nearly double in size (40 to 60 minutes).

5. Bake loaves in a 375° oven about 25 minutes or until golden brown and loaves sound hollow when lightly tapped. Brush with any remaining butter; cool. In a small bowl, combine powdered sugar and enough orange juice to reach drizzling consistency. Drizzle over loaves. **Makes 2 loaves (24 servings total).**

Per serving: 190 cal, 4 g fat, 27 mg chol, 110 mg sodium, 34 g carbo, 1 g fiber, 4 g pro.

Apple Scones with Spiced Maple Butter

Chopped apple inside and a thin slice of apple baked onto the top give this tender scone its fall flavor. They're shaped with a ¼-cup ice cream scoop.

PREP 30 minutes **BAKE** 15 minutes **COOL** 5 minutes

2¾ cups all-purpose flour
½ cup granulated sugar
1 tablespoon baking powder
1 teaspoon apple pie spice or ground cinnamon
½ teaspoon salt
½ cup butter, chilled and cut into small pieces
1 cup finely chopped tart apple (such as Braeburn, Jonagold or Jonathan)
2 eggs, lightly beaten
¾ cup whipping cream
1 egg yolk, beaten
1 tablespoon whipping cream
16 to 18 thin slices of unpeeled apple (such as Braeburn, Jonagold or Jonathan)
   Coarse sugar or granulated sugar
   Spiced Maple Butter or honey

1. Line an extra-large baking sheet with parchment paper or foil; set aside. In a large bowl, combine flour, sugar, baking powder, apple pie spice and salt. Using a pastry blender, cut in cold butter until mixture resembles coarse crumbs. Stir in the chopped apple. Make a well in center of flour mixture.

2. In a small bowl, combine the two eggs and ¾ cup whipping cream. Using a fork, stir egg mixture into flour mixture; stir until just moistened. Dough will be thick. Using a ¼-cup ice cream scoop or measuring cup, scoop dough into mounds and place on prepared baking sheet. Don't flatten.

3. In a small bowl, combine the egg yolk and 1 tablespoon whipping cream. Brush some of the mixture over the top of the dough mounds. Place an apple slice on top of each dough mound, pressing down until about 1 inch thick. Brush with remaining egg yolk mixture; sprinkle with coarse sugar.

4. Bake in a 375° oven for 15 to 17 minutes or until lightly browned. Cool on baking sheet on a wire rack for 5 minutes. Remove scones from baking sheet. Cool slightly. Serve warm with Spiced Maple Butter. **Makes 15 scones.**

Per scone: 297 cal, 18 g fat, 93 mg chol, 253 mg sodium, 30 g carbo, 1 g fiber, 4 g pro.

Spiced Maple Butter: In a small mixing bowl beat ½ cup softened butter, 2 tablespoons pure maple syrup or mild honey, and ¼ teaspoon apple pie spice with an electric mixer on medium speed until light and fluffy. Cover and chill for up to 1 week. Serve at room temperature. Makes ¾ cup.

Visit an orchard in the fall and find much more than apples. Many peddle slices of warm pie, cider and apple butter, too.

Maple-Sweet Potato Sticky Buns

In this new twist on cinnamon rolls, sweet potato adds a golden hue to these generous-size, tender sweet rolls that hint of maple syrup. Like most yeast bread, this recipe takes time to make, but it's worth it. Can't find hickory nuts? Substitute pecans or walnuts.

PREP 45 minutes   **RISE** 1 hour 30 minutes   **BAKE** 25 minutes   **COOL** 5 minutes

1 10- to 12- ounce sweet potato, peeled and cut up
5½ to 6 cups unbleached all-purpose flour or all-purpose flour
1 package active dry yeast
1 cup milk
⅓ cup maple syrup
⅓ cup butter
1 teaspoon salt
2 eggs
1 cup packed brown sugar
½ cup butter, softened
¼ cup maple syrup
3 tablespoons water
1 cup chopped hickory nuts, pecans or walnuts
¾ cup granulated sugar
¾ cup chopped hickory nuts, pecans or walnuts
⅓ cup butter, melted
1 tablespoon ground cinnamon
1 tablespoon unbleached all-purpose flour or all-purpose flour

1. In a covered medium saucepan, cook the sweet potato in enough boiling water to cover for 20 to 25 minutes or until soft; drain. Mash with a potato masher or fork. Measure 1 cup. Set aside. (For microwave: Prick unpeeled potato all over with a fork. Microwave on 100 percent power (high) for 5 to 7 minutes or until tender. Halve potato and scoop pulp out of skin into a small bowl; discard skin. Mash the potato.)

2. In a large mixing bowl, combine 2 cups of the flour and the yeast; set aside. In a medium saucepan, heat and stir milk, the 1 cup mashed potato, the ⅓ cup maple syrup, the ⅓ cup butter and salt just until warm (120° to 130°) and butter almost melts; add to flour mixture along with the eggs. Beat with an electric mixer on low to medium speed for 30 seconds, scraping sides of bowl constantly. Beat on high speed for 3 minutes. Using a wooden spoon, stir in as much of the remaining flour as you can.

3. Turn dough out onto a lightly floured surface. Knead in enough of the remaining flour to make a moderately soft dough that is smooth and elastic (3 to 5 minutes total). Shape dough into a ball. Place in a lightly greased bowl; turn once to grease surface of dough. Cover; let rise in a warm place until double in size (45 to 60 minutes).

4. Punch dough down. Turn dough out onto a lightly floured surface. Cover and let rest for 10 minutes. Meanwhile, lightly grease a 13x9x2-inch baking pan. Set aside.

5. In a medium bowl, whisk together brown sugar, the ½ cup softened butter, the ¼ cup maple syrup and the water until well combined (mixture may appear curdled). Spread in prepared pan. Sprinkle with the 1 cup nuts. Set aside.

6. For filling: In a small bowl, combine the granulated sugar, the ¾ cup nuts, the ⅓ cup melted butter, the cinnamon and the 1 tablespoon flour. Set aside.

7. Gently roll dough into an 18x12-inch rectangle. Crumble filling over dough, leaving 1 inch unfilled along one of the long sides. Carefully roll up rectangle, starting from the long filled side. Pinch dough edges to seal seams. With a serrated knife, slice dough roll crosswise into 12 equal pieces. Arrange evenly in four rows of three rolls each, cut sides down, in prepared pan. Cover loosely with buttered plastic wrap and let rise in a warm place until nearly double in size (about 45 minutes).

8. Uncover rolls. Bake in a 375° oven for 25 to 30 minutes or until golden, tenting loosely with foil if buns begin to brown too quickly. Place a large baking sheet on the rack below the baking pan. Cool in pan on a wire rack for 5 minutes. Invert onto a large tray or serving platter. Serve warm. **Makes 12 buns.**

Make-ahead tip: Prepare as above through Step 7, except do not let rise after shaping. Cover loosely with oiled waxed paper, then with plastic wrap. Chill for 2 to 24 hours. Before baking, let chilled rolls stand, covered, for 30 minutes at room temperature. Uncover and bake as directed.

Per bun: 689 cal, 31 g fat, 84 mg chol, 362 mg sodium, 95 g carbo, 4 g fiber, 11 g pro.

PUMPKIN-CURRANT
SCONES AND
GARLIC AND
ROSEMARY KNOTS

Pumpkin-Currant Scones

PREP 25 minutes **BAKE** 12 minutes

- 2½ cups all-purpose flour
- ¾ cup packed brown sugar
- 1 tablespoon ground ginger
- 1 tablespoon ground cinnamon
- 2 teaspoons baking powder
- ½ teaspoon salt
- ½ teaspoon baking soda
- ½ teaspoon ground nutmeg
- ¼ teaspoon ground cloves
- ½ cup cold unsalted butter, cut into pieces (no substitutes)
- 2 eggs
- ¾ cup canned pumpkin
- ½ cup dried currants or snipped raisins
- ½ cup buttermilk
- ½ teaspoon vanilla
- 1 beaten egg white
- 1 tablespoon water
  Granulated sugar

1. In a large mixing bowl, combine flour, brown sugar, ginger, cinnamon, baking powder, salt, soda, nutmeg and cloves. Using a pastry blender, cut in butter until mixture resembles coarse crumbs. Make a well in center of flour mixture; set aside.

2. In a medium mixing bowl, combine eggs, pumpkin, currants, buttermilk and vanilla. Add egg mixture all at once to flour mixture. Stir just until combined. Do not overmix.

3. Drop dough in ¼-cup portions 2 inches apart on ungreased baking sheets. In a small bowl, combine beaten egg white and the water. Lightly brush egg white mixture over the scones; sprinkle with granulated sugar. Bake in a 400° oven for 12 to 14 minutes or until lightly browned. Remove scones from baking sheet; serve warm. To reheat, wrap scones in foil; heat in a 400° oven for 5 to 8 minutes. **Makes 20 scones.**

Per scone: 164 cal, 6 g fat, 35 mg chol, 151 mg sodium, 26 g carbo, 1 g fiber, 3 g pro.

Best Potato Rolls

PREP 40 minutes **RISE** 1 hour 20 minutes **BAKE** 15 minutes **STAND** 10 minutes

- 2 small russet (baking) potatoes (12 ounces total), peeled and cut into chunks
- 1 cup buttermilk
- ¼ cup butter
- 2 tablespoons sugar
- 2 teaspoons salt
- 5 to 5¾ cups bread flour or all-purpose flour
- 2 packages active dry yeast
- 2 tablespoons butter, melted

1. In a small saucepan, cook potatoes, covered, in enough boiling water to cover for 15 to 20 minutes or until tender; drain, reserving ½ cup of the cooking liquid. Using a fork, mash the potatoes; set aside. Add buttermilk, the ¼ cup butter, the sugar and salt to the hot cooking liquid; heat until warm (120° to 130°) and butter is almost melted.

2. In a large mixing bowl, stir together 1½ cups of the flour and the yeast. Stir in the buttermilk mixture and mashed potatoes. Beat with an electric mixer on low speed for 30 seconds, scraping bowl constantly. Beat on high speed for 3 minutes. Stir in as much of the remaining flour as you can.

3. Turn dough out onto a lightly floured surface. Knead in enough of the remaining flour to make a moderately stiff dough that is smooth and elastic (6 to 8 minutes total). Shape dough into a ball. Place in a buttered bowl; turn once. Cover; let rise in a warm place until double (about 1 hour).

4. Punch dough down. Turn dough out onto a lightly floured surface. Divide dough in half. Cover; let rest for 10 minutes. Meanwhile, lightly grease three baking sheets (or line baking sheets with parchment paper).

5. On a lightly floured surface, roll each portion of dough into a 10x6-inch rectangle (¾-inch thick). Cut each rectangle of dough into fifteen 2-inch squares. Place squares 2 to 3 inches apart on the prepared baking sheets. Brush tops with the 2 tablespoons melted butter. Cover with plastic wrap; let rise in a warm place for 15 minutes.

6. Bake in a 375° oven 15 to 18 minutes or until golden. Immediately remove rolls from baking sheet. Cool slightly on a rack. Serve warm. **Makes 30 rolls.**

Garlic and Rosemary Knots: Prepare as above. Cut each rectangle of dough into fifteen 6x¾-inch strips. Gently pull strips into 8-inch-long ropes. In a small bowl, combine ¾ cup olive oil, 3 tablespoons snipped fresh rosemary and 2 cloves garlic, minced. Dip each rope into oil mixture. Tie in a loose knot. Place knots 2 to 3 inches apart on the prepared baking sheets. Sprinkle with coarse or kosher salt. Cover with plastic wrap; let rise in a warm place for 15 minutes. Bake in a 375° oven about 15 minutes or until golden. Immediately remove rolls from baking sheet. Cool slightly on a rack. Serve warm. **Makes 30 knots.**

Per roll: 118 cal, 3 g fat, 7 mg chol, 190 mg sodium, 19 g carbo, 1 g fiber, 3 g pro.

The BMC²

The Chicago pharmacist who developed this recipe used a scientific-formula approach to name this sweet-salty muffin with cinnamon swirl and maple frosting, topped with sauteed apples and bacon: Bacon, maple syrup and cinnamon (squared).

PREP 35 minutes   **BAKE** 20 minutes   **COOL** 10 minutes

Cinnamon Filling (recipe follows)
1¾ cups all-purpose flour
1½ teaspoons baking powder
½ teaspoon salt
½ cup butter, softened
½ cup sugar
1 egg
½ teaspoon vanilla
½ cup milk
Maple Cream Cheese Frosting (recipe follows)
Sauteed Apples (recipe follows)
Crumbled, crisp-cooked applewood smoked bacon

1. Line twelve 2½-inch muffin cups with paper bake cups; set aside. Prepare Cinnamon Filling. Set aside.

2. In a small bowl, combine flour, baking powder and salt. In a large mixing bowl, beat butter with an electric mixer on medium to high speed for 30 seconds. Gradually add sugar, beating just until combined. Add egg and vanilla; beat just until combined. Alternately add the flour mixture and milk, beating on low speed after each addition.

3. Spoon 2 tablespoons batter into each of the paper-lined muffin cups. Spoon 1 rounded teaspoon of the filling onto batter in each cup. Top with remaining batter.

4. Bake in a 350° oven for 20 to 25 minutes or until tops spring back when lightly touched. Cool in pan on a wire rack for 10 minutes. Remove muffins from pan.

5. Spread Maple Cream Cheese Frosting over muffins. Spoon Sauteed Apples on top of frosting and sprinkle with bacon. Serve warm. Store any leftover muffins in the refrigerator. **Makes 12 muffins.**

Per muffin: 506 cal, 20 g fat, 73 mg chol, 345 mg sodium, 78 g carbo, 1 g fiber, 5 g pro.

Cinnamon Filling: In a small bowl, combine ⅓ cup packed brown sugar; ⅓ cup butter, melted; 1 tablespoon flour; and 1 tablespoon ground cinnamon.

Maple Cream Cheese Frosting: In a large mixing bowl, beat together one 8-ounce package reduced-fat cream cheese (Neufchâtel) and 1 tablespoon pure maple syrup with an electric mixer on medium speed until light and fluffy. Gradually beat in 4 cups powdered sugar just until combined.

Sauteed Apples: Peel, core and chop 3 medium apples. In a large skillet, cook chopped apples in 2 tablespoons hot butter over medium heat for 5 minutes or until tender. Sprinkle with 2 tablespoons sugar. Cook and stir until sugar is dissolved.

BUFFALO CHICKEN
WINGS WITH BLUE
CHEESE DRESSING

Buffalo Chicken Wings with Blue Cheese Dressing

Love wings? Here's a heart-healthy way to make them (don't worry, they taste just as good as the original). Dip these wings in a kicky dressing of blue cheese, garlic powder, vinegar and spicy cayenne pepper sauce.

START TO FINISH 30 minutes

- 24 chicken drummettes, skinned*
- ¼ cup bottled cayenne pepper sauce
- 2 teaspoons cider vinegar
- ½ teaspoon garlic powder
- ½ teaspoon ground ginger
- ¾ cup fat-free sour cream
- ½ cup crumbled blue cheese
- 1 green onion, chopped
- 1 tablespoon white wine vinegar
- 1 tablespoon lemon juice
- 1 teaspoon sugar
  Carrot sticks
  Celery sticks

1. In a large bowl, toss the drummettes with 2 tablespoons of the cayenne pepper sauce, 1 teaspoon of the cider vinegar, the garlic powder and ginger.

2. Arrange drummettes on the unheated rack of a broiler pan. Broil 4 to 5 inches from the heat for 15 to 20 minutes or until chicken is tender and no longer pink, turning once. Drizzle chicken with the remaining 2 tablespoons cayenne pepper sauce and 1 teaspoon cider vinegar.

3. Meanwhile, for dressing in a small bowl, combine sour cream, blue cheese, green onion, white wine vinegar, lemon juice and sugar. Serve dressing and carrot and celery sticks with chicken drummettes. **Makes 8 servings.**

*Note: Grasp the edge of the skin with a paper towel and pull it away from the drummette.

Per serving: 112 cal, 4 g fat, 24 mg chol, 216 mg sodium, 10 g carbo, 2 g fiber, 9 g pro.

Habanero Hot Wings

If you can't find the ground habanero chile pepper at your supermarket, look at a Mexican market. But beware. It's very hot! If you like hot stuff, use the ½ teaspoon. Scale back if you're a milder soul.

PREP 25 minutes **BAKE** 45 minutes

  Nonstick cooking spray
- 2 tablespoons onion powder
- 1 tablespoon garlic powder
- 2 teaspoons smoked paprika or sweet paprika
- 2 teaspoons dried cilantro, crushed
- 1 teaspoon dry mustard
- ½ teaspoon chili powder
- ¼ to ½ teaspoon ground habanero chile pepper
- 12 chicken wings (about 2 pounds)
- ½ cup bottled hickory barbecue sauce
- 2 tablespoons peach spreadable fruit or desired fruit preserves (such as peach, pineapple or orange)
- 1 tablespoon bottled steak sauce or ketchup
  Dill Dipping Sauce, Celery Dipping Sauce or Feta Dipping Sauce (recipes follow)

1. Coat a 15x10x1-inch baking pan with cooking spray; set aside. For seasoning: In a resealable plastic bag, combine onion powder, garlic powder, paprika, cilantro, mustard, chili powder and the ¼ teaspoon habanero chile pepper; set aside.

2. Cut off and discard tips of chicken wings. Cut wings at joints to form 24 pieces. Place chicken wing pieces in a plastic bag with seasoning mixture. Seal bag; toss to coat wings with seasoning mixture. Arrange wings in prepared pan. Bake in a 375° oven for 25 minutes.

3. For sauce, in a small saucepan, combine barbecue sauce, spreadable fruit and steak sauce. Cook and stir over medium heat until the ingredients are blended; set aside.

4. Carefully brush wings with half of the sauce. Turn wings and brush with the remaining sauce. Bake for 20 to 25 minutes more or until chicken is tender and no longer pink. Serve with your choice of Dipping Sauces and remaining barbecue sauce mixture. **Makes 12 appetizer servings.**

Dill Dipping Sauce: In a small bowl, combine ¾ cup mayonnaise, ¼ cup plain yogurt, and 1 teaspoon snipped fresh dill or ¼ teaspoon dried dillweed.

Celery Dipping Sauce: Prepare Dill Dipping Sauce as above, except substitute 1 teaspoon celery seeds for the dill.

Feta Dipping Sauce: Prepare Dill Dipping Sauce as above, except substitute ½ cup crumbled feta cheese or blue cheese for the dill.

Per serving: 223 cal, 18 g fat, 37 mg chol, 274 mg sodium, 7 g carbo, 0 g fiber, 8 g pro.

Toasted Ravioli

Stories say a cook in St. Louis' Italian Hill neighborhood dropped cooked raviolis into hot oil. The world has been enjoying dropping the crispy appetizer into tomato sauce ever since.

PREP 25 minutes **COOK** 30 minutes **FRY** 2 minutes per batch

¼ cup finely chopped onion
1 clove garlic, minced
1 tablespoon olive oil or butter
2 pounds ripe fresh tomatoes, peeled, seeded and cut up
2 tablespoons snipped fresh basil or 1 teaspoon dried basil, crushed
½ teaspoon salt
⅛ teaspoon ground black pepper
2 tablespoons tomato paste
2 eggs, lightly beaten
¼ cup milk
16 to 20 frozen meat-filled ravioli, thawed
1 to 1⅓ cups seasoned fine dry bread crumbs
Vegetable oil for deep-fat frying
Grated Parmesan cheese (optional)

1. For sauce, in a medium saucepan, cook onion and garlic in hot olive oil over medium heat until onion is tender. Stir in tomatoes, dried basil (if using), salt and pepper. Cook, covered, about 10 minutes or until tomatoes are soft, stirring occasionally.

2. Stir in tomato paste. Bring to boiling; reduce heat. Simmer, uncovered, about 20 minutes or until sauce reaches desired consistency, stirring occasionally. Stir in fresh basil, if using. Cover and keep warm.

3. Meanwhile, in a small bowl, combine eggs and milk. Dip each ravioli into egg mixture, then into bread crumbs to coat.

4. In a heavy 3-quart saucepan, heat 2 inches of vegetable oil to 350°. Fry ravioli, a few at a time, in hot oil about 2 minutes or until golden brown, turning once. Using a slotted spoon, remove from hot oil and drain on paper towels. Keep warm in a 300° oven while frying the remaining ravioli.

5. To serve, sprinkle ravioli with Parmesan, if you like. Serve with warm sauce for dipping. **Makes 12 to 14 servings.**

Note: If you like, use purchased spaghetti sauce or pizza sauce for dipping instead of making the homemade tomato sauce.

Per serving: 195 cal, 10 g fat, 55 mg chol, 417 mg sodium, 21 g carbo, 2 g fiber, 7 g pro.

When the air turns cool and paints the leaves warm shades of color, we welcome friends and family with hearty, comforting foods.

SLIM TEX-MEX
TACO DIP

Slim Tex-Mex Taco Dip

PREP 30 minutes **BAKE** 25 minutes

- 1½ pounds ground raw turkey breast
- 1 jalapeño chile pepper, seeded and finely chopped (optional; see Note, page 58)
- 1 1-ounce envelope reduced-sodium taco seasoning mix
- 2 8-ounce packages reduced-fat cream cheese (Neufchâtel), softened
- 2 16-ounce cans fat-free refried beans
- 2 tablespoons lemon juice
- 3 avocados, halved, seeded, peeled and mashed
- ½ cup fat-free dairy sour cream
- ½ cup fat-free mayonnaise
- 8 ounces reduced-fat shredded cheddar cheese
- ½ cup chopped green onions (optional)
- 2 cups shredded fresh spinach
- 3 medium tomatoes, chopped
  Assorted vegetable dippers and/or baked tortilla chips

1. In a large skillet, cook ground turkey and jalapeño, if using, with half of the taco seasoning mix (about 2 tablespoons) until turkey is no longer pink; remove from heat and set aside.

2. Meanwhile, spread cream cheese into the bottom of a 13x9x2-inch baking dish. Spread cream cheese layer with refried beans. Stir the lemon juice into the mashed avocados and spread over refried bean layer. In a small bowl, stir together sour cream, mayonnaise and remaining taco seasoning mix. Spread this sour cream mixture atop the avocado layer. Top with ground turkey mixture, and then sprinkle with cheese.

3. Bake, uncovered, in a 325° oven about 25 minutes or until heated through and cheese is evenly melted. Top with green onions, if you like, shredded spinach and chopped tomatoes. Serve with vegetable dippers and/or baked tortilla chips. **Makes 24 servings.**

Per serving: 175 cal, 9 g fat, 32 mg chol, 425 mg sodium, 10 g carbo, 3 g fiber, 13 g pro.

Gouda and Red Onion Pizza

PREP 25 minutes **BAKE** 12 minutes

- 2 tablespoons olive oil
- 1 large red onion, halved lengthwise and thinly sliced (about 2 cups)
- 1 tablespoon snipped fresh thyme or 1 teaspoon dried thyme, crushed
- ¼ teaspoon salt
- ¼ teaspoon freshly ground black pepper
- 1 tablespoon cornmeal
- 1 13.8-ounce can refrigerated pizza dough
- 8 ounces Gouda or Edam cheese, shredded (2 cups)

1. In a large skillet, heat 1 tablespoon oil over medium heat. Add onion. Cook until onion is tender but not brown, stirring often (5 to 7 minutes). Remove from heat. Stir in thyme, salt and black pepper; set aside.

2. Grease a baking sheet and sprinkle with the cornmeal. Pat pizza dough into a 12x8-inch rectangle on the baking sheet. Brush pizza dough with remaining 1 tablespoon oil. Sprinkle pizza dough with cheese to within ½ inch of edges. Spoon onion mixture over the cheese.

3. Bake, uncovered, in a 400° oven for 12 to 15 minutes or until crust is golden. Cut into 12 pieces. **Makes 12 appetizer servings.**

Per serving: 146 cal, 8 g fat, 21 mg chol, 278 mg sodium, 11 g carbo, 1 g fiber, 6 g pro.

Jack Cheese and Smoky Chipotle Fondue

PREP 30 minutes **COOK** 20 minutes

  4 slices bacon, halved crosswise
  ¼ cup finely chopped green onions
  ¼ cup finely chopped red or yellow sweet pepper
  2 cloves garlic, minced
  2 teaspoons all-purpose flour
  4 cups shredded Monterey Jack cheese (16 ounces)
  2 8-ounce cartons dairy sour cream
  2 to 3 teaspoons finely chopped chipotle peppers in adobo sauce
    French or Italian bread, cut into bite-size cubes
    Tortilla chips or tortilla chip cups

1. In a heavy, medium saucepan, cook bacon until crisp. Remove bacon; reserving 1 tablespoon drippings in pan. Drain bacon on paper towels; crumble bacon and set aside.

2. Add green onions, ¼ cup sweet pepper and garlic to saucepan. Cook and stir onion mixture over medium heat about 5 minutes or until vegetables are tender. Stir in flour. Stir in cheese, sour cream and chipotle peppers. Cook and stir over medium-low heat until cheese is melted and mixture is smooth.

3. Transfer cheese mixture to fondue pot. Top with crumbled bacon. Place over a fondue burner; keep warm up to 2 hours. Spear bread cubes with fondue forks; dip in fondue, swirling to coat. Or dip tortilla chips in fondue. **Makes 16 (¼-cup) servings.**

Per serving: 186 cal, 16 g fat, 40 mg chol, 200 mg sodium, 2 g carbo, 0 g fiber, 8 g pro.

Slow-Cooker Sweet-Hot Nuts

PREP 15 minutes **COOK** 2 hours on low **COOL** 1 hour

  1 cup whole cashews
  1 cup whole almonds, toasted*
  1 cup pecan halves, toasted*
  1 cup hazelnuts, toasted and skins removed*
  ½ cup sugar
  ⅓ cup butter, melted
  1 teaspoon ground ginger
  ½ teaspoon salt
  ½ teaspoon ground cinnamon
  ¼ teaspoon ground cloves
  ¼ teaspoon cayenne pepper

1. Place nuts in a 2- to 3½-quart slow cooker. In a small bowl, combine sugar, butter, ginger, salt, cinnamon, cloves and cayenne pepper. Add nuts to slow cooker; toss to coat.

2. Cover and cook on low-heat setting for 2 hours, stirring after 1 hour. Stir nuts again. Spread in a single layer on buttered foil; let cool for at least 1 hour. (Nuts may appear soft after cooking but will crisp upon cooling.) Store in a tightly covered container at room temperature for up to 3 weeks. **Makes 22 (¼ cup) servings.**

*Note: To toast nuts, spread nuts in a single layer in a shallow baking pan. Bake in a 350° oven for 10 to 15 minutes or until light golden brown, watching carefully and stirring once or twice. To remove the papery skin from hazelnuts, rub the nuts with a clean dish towel.

Per serving: 147 cal, 13 g fat, 7 mg chol, 73 mg sodium, 8 g carbo, 2 g fiber, 3 g pro.

With the arrival of fall, the season of holiday celebration and entertaining begins in earnest. To please the crowds, look to simple, surefire recipes like fondue and toasted nuts.

SLOW-COOKER
SWEET-HOT NUTS

A visit to a pick-your-own pumpkin patch is an autumn ritual for many Midwest families. Taking a hayrack ride out to the field to search for the perfect pumpkin for pie or for carving a Halloween jack-o'-lantern is so much fun.

Beef Short Ribs with Cranberry-Port Gravy

PREP 25 minutes COOK 8 to 10 hours on low or 4 to 5 hours on high

- 3 tablespoons olive oil
- 4 pounds bone-in beef short ribs with bone (use boneless if bone-in is not available)
- 2 tablespoons crushed green peppercorns
- 2 teaspoons kosher salt
- 1 large red onion, sliced
- 1 14-ounce can whole cranberry sauce
- 1 14-ounce can beef broth
- 3 tablespoons snipped fresh rosemary
- 3 tablespoons lemon juice
- ¼ cup cold water
- 2 tablespoons cornstarch
- ¼ cup port
- 3 cups cooked wild rice
  Fresh rosemary sprigs

1. In a large nonstick skillet, heat oil over medium-high heat. Sprinkle ribs with peppercorns and salt. Cook, in batches, in hot oil about 5 minutes or until brown on all sides. Place ribs in a 6-quart slow cooker. Place onion slices on top of ribs. In a medium bowl, combine cranberry sauce, beef broth, rosemary and lemon juice. Pour over ribs. Cover and cook on low for 8 to 10 hours or on high for 4 to 5 hours. Transfer ribs to a warm dish; cover to keep warm.

2. For gravy: Strain cooking liquid and skim off fat. Place the liquid in a medium saucepan; bring to boiling. Stir together the cold water and cornstarch. Stir into boiling liquid; reduce heat. Cook and stir about 2 minutes or until mixture is slightly thickened. Add port; cook and stir for 1 minute more. Remove from heat.

3. Place wild rice on a serving platter. Top with ribs and some of the gravy. Garnish with fresh rosemary. Pass remaining gravy. **Makes 6 to 8 servings.**

Per serving: 760 cal, 55 g fat, 114 mg chol, 670 mg sodium, 38 g carbo, 2 g fiber, 27 g pro.

Wagyu Beef Carbonnade

PREP 35 minutes COOK 2 hours

- 1 3-pound American Wagyu chuck roast or boneless beef chuck arm pot roast, cut into 3-inch cubes
- 1 tablespoon vegetable oil
- 4 ounces pancetta (Italian bacon) or sliced bacon, chopped
- 2 yellow onions, thinly sliced
- ½ cup tomato paste (4 ounces)
- 8 cloves garlic, minced
- 2 12-ounce bottles good quality dark stout, dark or porter beer (or nonalcoholic beer)
- 4 cups chicken broth
- 2 bay leaves
  Hot cooked and buttered noodles, spätzle, gnocchi, mashed potatoes or polenta
  Kosher salt (optional)

1. In a 4- to 6-quart Dutch oven, brown half of the beef cubes on all sides in hot oil over medium-high heat. (Make sure to get a good sear, as this will add flavor to the finished dish.) Using a slotted spoon, remove beef from pan; set aside. Brown the remaining beef cubes; remove from pan. Reserve the pan drippings.

2. In the same pan, cook pancetta over medium heat just until it starts to brown. Remove and add to the beef, reserving pan drippings.

3. In the same pan, cook onions over medium heat for 6 to 8 minutes or until tender but not brown, stirring frequently. Add tomato paste and garlic. Cook and stir for 4 minutes. Add beer. Bring to boiling, stirring constantly. Add beef, pancetta, broth and bay leaves. Return to boiling; reduce heat. Simmer, partially covered, for 2 to 3 hours or until the beef is fork-tender and the sauce has thickened slightly.

4. To serve, remove bay leaves; discard. If you like, use a fork to break up beef cubes. Spoon beef mixture over hot cooked and buttered noodles. Salt to taste, if you like. **Makes 8 servings.**

Note: To reheat, simmer over low heat, adding water if necessary.

Per serving: 584 cal, 31 g fat, 117 mg chol, 776 mg sodium, 36 g carbo, 3 g fiber, 34 g pro.

The hearty foods of fall—succulent braised beef dishes among them—warm you up from the inside out. Long slow-cooking makes for the tenderest texture and best flavor and gives the chef time to do other things.

**WAGYU BEEF
CARBONNADE**

Pasties

When miners in Michigan's Upper Peninsula carried these meat-and-veggie pies in their pockets, they counted on sturdy crusts. Our version is a little more tender and moist. But it still tastes great eaten the traditional way—drenched in gravy or ketchup.

PREP 30 minutes **BAKE** 20 minutes

Pastry for a Single-Crust Pie (recipe follows)

⅔ cup cooked chopped or ground beef, pork, lamb, chicken and/or turkey

⅔ cup chopped cooked potato, sweet potato, carrot, turnip and/or rutabaga; cooked corn or cooked peas

¼ cup chopped onion

2 tablespoons steak sauce

Milk

Ketchup, pizza sauce, barbecue sauce or sour cream

1. Prepare Pastry for a Single-Crust Pie. Divide dough into four portions. On a lightly floured surface, use your hands to slightly flatten a portion of the dough. Roll dough from center to edge into a 6-inch circle. Repeat with remaining dough portions.

2. For filling, in a small bowl, combine meat, vegetable, onion and steak sauce.

3. Spoon about ⅓ cup of the filling onto half of each pastry circle. Lightly moisten edge with a little milk. Fold other half of pastry over filling. Seal edges by crimping with a fork. Cut slits in pastry to allow steam to escape. Brush with a little additional milk. Place on an ungreased large baking sheet.

4. Bake in a 375° oven for 20 to 25 minutes or until pastry is golden brown. Cool slightly on wire racks. Serve warm with ketchup. **Makes 4 servings.**

Pastry for a Single-Crust Pie: In a medium bowl, stir together 1½ cups all-purpose flour and ½ teaspoon salt. Using a pastry blender, cut in ¼ cup shortening and ¼ cup butter, cut up, or shortening until pieces are pea-size. Sprinkle 1 tablespoon ice water over part of the flour mixture; gently toss with a fork. Push moistened pastry to the side of the bowl. Repeat moistening flour mixture, using 1 tablespoon ice water at a time, until all of the flour mixture is moistened (¼ to ⅓ cup ice water total). Gather flour mixture into a ball, kneading gently until it holds together.

Note: To save time, use half of a 15-ounce package (one crust) rolled refrigerated unbaked piecrust instead of the homemade pastry. Let stand according to package directions. Unroll and cut into four pieces. Roll each into a 6-inch circle.

Per serving: 525 cal, 29 g fat, 56 mg chol, 879 mg sodium, 50 g carbo, 2 g fiber, 14 g pro.

Italian Beef Sandwiches

The variation with cheese is known as a "cheesy beef" at the family-style restaurants and sandwich stands in Chicago, where this sandwich is said to have been born in the late 1930s.

PREP 25 minutes **COOK** 10 to 11 hours on low or 5 to 5½ hours on high

1 4-pound boneless beef sirloin or beef rump roast, cut into 2- to 3-inch pieces
½ cup water
1 0.7-ounce envelope Italian dry salad dressing mix
2 teaspoons dried Italian seasoning, crushed
½ to 1 teaspoon crushed red pepper
½ teaspoon garlic powder
10 to 12 hoagie buns, kaiser rolls or other sandwich rolls, split
1½ cups shredded Italian blend cheeses (6 ounces) (optional)
Pickles, sliced onion, sliced pepperoncini, roasted red sweet pepper strips, and/or giardiniera (optional)

1. Place beef in a 4- or 5-quart slow cooker. In a small bowl, combine the water, salad dressing mix, Italian seasoning, crushed red pepper and garlic powder; pour over beef in slow cooker. Cover and cook on low-heat setting for 10 to 11 hours or on high-heat setting for 5 to 5½ hours.

2. Remove meat from cooker with a slotted spoon. Using two forks, shred the meat. Serve meat in rolls. If you like, sprinkle sandwiches with cheese and place sandwiches on two large baking sheets; broil sandwiches, one pan at a time, 4 to 5 inches from the heat for 1 to 2 minutes or until cheese is melted.

3. Strain cooking juices through a fine-mesh sieve. Drizzle each sandwich with some of the strained juices to moisten. If you like, top each sandwich with pickles, sliced onion, sliced pepperoncini and/or roasted red sweet pepper strips or giardiniera. Serve remaining cooking juices for dipping, if you like. **Makes 10 to 12 servings.**

Per serving: 564 cal, 19 g fat, 117 mg chol, 921 mg sodium, 51 g carbo, 2 g fiber, 44 g pro.

This classic Chicago sandwich can be served two ways: Sweet (with Italian sweet peppers) or hot (with giardiniera, a melange of pickled hot pepper and vegetables.).

Cincinnati-Style Chili

PREP 25 minutes **COOK** 1 hour

5 bay leaves
1 teaspoon whole allspice
½ teaspoon whole cloves
2 pounds ground beef
2 cups chopped onions (2 large)
2 cloves garlic, minced
2 tablespoons chili powder
1 teaspoon ground cinnamon
½ teaspoon cayenne pepper
⅛ teaspoon ground cardamom
2 14-ounce cans beef broth or 3½ cups water
1 15- to 16-ounce can red kidney beans, rinsed and drained
1 8-ounce can tomato sauce
1 tablespoon vinegar
1 teaspoon Worcestershire sauce
¼ teaspoon salt
12 ounces dried spaghetti, cooked and drained
Shredded cheddar cheese (optional)
Chopped onion (optional)
Oyster crackers (optional)

1. For spice bag: Place bay leaves, allspice and cloves in a double-thick, 6-inch square of 100-percent-cotton cheesecloth. Bring up corners; tie closed with kitchen string.

2. For meat sauce: In a 4- to 5-quart Dutch oven, cook beef, 2 cups onions and the garlic until meat is brown and onion is tender. Drain off fat.

3. Stir in chili powder, cinnamon, cayenne pepper and cardamom. Cook and stir for 1 minute. Stir in broth, drained beans, tomato sauce, vinegar, Worcestershire sauce and salt. Add spice bag. Bring to boiling; reduce heat. Simmer, covered, for 45 minutes. Simmer, uncovered, about 15 minutes more or until sauce reaches desired consistency. Remove spice bag; discard.

4. To serve, top hot spaghetti with meat sauce. If you like, sprinkle with cheese and additional onion, and serve with oyster crackers. **Makes 6 to 8 servings.**

Per serving: 761 cal, 40 g fat, 113 mg chol, 1046 mg sodium, 64 g carbo, 8 g fiber, 39 g pro.

A couple of things identify chili as being Cincinnati-style. One is the flavoring. It can contain cinnamon, cardamom, cloves—even chocolate. The other is the bed of spaghetti on which it is served. The story goes that it was invented by an immigrant restaurateur from Eastern Europe who wanted to broaden his audience by selling more than his own ethnic style of cuisine.

Ultimate Grilled Cheese and Ham Panini with Parsnip Fries

Sweet-tart fruit meets savory-salty ham and cheese in this grilled sandwich.

PREP 25 minutes **COOK** 6 minutes

1 16-ounce loaf unsliced ciabatta or Italian bread or 8 slices French, sourdough, multigrain or oatmeal bread, sliced ½ to ¾ inch thick

½ cup chutney (you choose the flavor)

3 ounces thinly sliced Fontina, Jarlsberg, Gruyére or Swiss cheese

8 ounces thinly sliced cooked ham

1 small Bosc or Anjou pear or 1 small apple, cored and thinly sliced

1 cup fresh baby arugula or spinach

3 ounces thinly sliced Gouda, Edam, Muenster or provolone cheese

2 to 3 tablespoons butter, softened, or olive oil

Parsnip Fries (recipe follows) or potato chips (optional)

1. If using bread loaf, carefully trim off and discard the top crust of the bread to make a flat surface, if necessary. Turn bread over; trim off and discard bottom crust, if necessary. Cut remaining bread loaf in half horizontally to form two ½-inch-thick slices.

2. Preheat an electric sandwich press, a covered indoor grill, a grill pan or a 12-inch skillet over medium-low heat for 1 to 2 minutes.

3. If needed, snip any large pieces of chutney. Spread chutney on one side of each slice of bread. Place the Fontina cheese on half of the loaf or on four of the bread slices. Top with ham, pear, arugula, the Gouda cheese and the other half of bread loaf or remaining slices. Spread both sides of loaf or sandwiches evenly with butter or brush with oil. Cut loaf crosswise into four sandwiches.

4. Place sandwiches (two at a time, if necessary) in the sandwich press or indoor grill. Cover and cook for 6 to 8 minutes or until bread is toasted and cheese melted. (If using a grill pan or skillet, place sandwiches in pan. Weight sandwiches down with a heavy skillet or a pie plate containing a can of vegetables. Cook until bread is lightly toasted. Using hot pads, carefully remove top skillet. Turn sandwiches over, weight down, and cook until bread is toasted and cheese is melted.) If you like, serve sandwiches with Parsnip Fries. **Makes 4 sandwiches.**

Per sandwich: 659 cal, 25 g fat, 101 mg chol, 1,867 mg sodium, 78 g carbo, 4 g fiber, 30 g pro.

Parsnip Fries: Peel 4 medium parsnips; cut into ⅛-inch-thick lengthwise slices using a mandolin slicer or cut by hand. Place parsnip slices in a large bowl of ice water; let soak for 10 minutes. Drain parsnips and thoroughly pat dry with paper towels. In a 3-quart saucepan or an electric deep-fat fryer, heat 2 inches of vegetable or peanut oil to 375°. Fry parsnips, one-fourth at a time, about 1 to 2 minutes or until golden brown and crisp. Remove parsnips from the hot oil using a slotted spoon; drain on paper towels. Sprinkle with kosher salt. Transfer parsnips to a wire rack set on a baking sheet, arranging them in a single layer. Keep warm in a 300° oven. Makes 3 cups.

Harvest Chipotle Chili

Spiced nuts and tart apples make a surprise appearance in this autumnal version of a Midwest favorite.

PREP 30 minutes **COOK** 25 minutes

3 medium orange sweet peppers, halved and seeded
2 canned chipotle peppers in adobo sauce
2 cloves garlic
1½ pounds ground pork, ground beef or uncooked ground turkey or chicken
1 large onion, chopped (1 cup)
1 pound sweet potato, peeled and cut into 1-inch pieces
1 15-ounce can reduced-sodium pinto beans, rinsed and drained
1 14.5-ounce can hominy or one 15.5-ounce can butter beans, rinsed and drained
1 14.5-ounce can chunky chili-style tomatoes or stewed tomatoes, undrained
1 12-ounce can beer or one 14.5-ounce can reduced-sodium chicken broth
1 14.5-ounce can reduced-sodium chicken broth
2 medium Granny Smith or tart red apples, peeled, cored and coarsely chopped
1 teaspoon kosher salt
Spicy Chipotle Seasoned Nuts (recipe follows; optional) or ½ cup coarsely chopped dry-roasted cashews

1. In a food processor, cover and process sweet peppers, chipotle peppers and garlic with on/off turns until finely chopped. Set aside.

2. In an 8-quart Dutch oven, cook ground pork and onion over medium-high heat until meat is brown and onion is tender, breaking up meat as it cooks. Drain off fat. Add pepper-garlic mixture; cook and stir for 5 minutes.

3. Stir in the sweet potato, pinto beans, drained hominy, undrained tomatoes, beer, chicken broth, apples and salt. Bring to boiling; reduce heat. Simmer, covered, for 25 to 30 minutes or until sweet potato is tender.

4. Top each serving with some of the Spicy Chipotle Seasoned Nuts. **Makes 8 servings.**

Spicy Chipotle Seasoned Nuts: Line a 13x9x2-inch baking pan with foil; lightly coat foil with nonstick cooking spray. Set aside. In a small saucepan, combine 2 tablespoons butter, 2 teaspoons Worcestershire sauce, 1 teaspoon water, 1 teaspoon ground chipotle chile pepper or chili powder, 1 teaspoon snipped fresh rosemary, ½ teaspoon celery salt and ½ teaspoon garlic powder. Cook and stir over low heat until the butter is melted. Simmer over very low heat for 2 minutes to combine flavors. Stir in 1½ cups dry-roasted cashews, unsalted pumpkin seeds (pepitas) and/or peanuts. Spread nut mixture in an even layer in the prepared pan. Bake in a 325° oven for 15 to 20 minutes, stirring twice. Sprinkle ½ teaspoon kosher, sea salt or coarse salt over warm nuts, stirring to coat. Remove foil with nuts from pan; set aside to cool. Store in an airtight container or bag for up to 2 weeks. (This makes a great snack—double the recipe and keep half for the chili.) Makes 1½ cups.

Per serving: 424 cal, 19 g fat, 61 mg chol, 866 mg sodium, 40 g carbo, 8 g fiber, 21 g pro.

Pulled Pork Sandwiches with Root Beer Barbecue Sauce

Root beer, the surprise ingredient, adds sweetness to the roast as it cooks and to the sweet, dark sauce.

PREP 25 minutes **COOK** 8 to 10 hours on low or 4 to 5 hours on high

- 1 2½- to 3-pound boneless pork sirloin roast
- ½ teaspoon salt
- ½ teaspoon ground black pepper
- 1 tablespoon vegetable oil
- 2 medium onions, cut into thin wedges
- 1 cup root beer
- 2 tablespoons minced garlic
- 3 cups root beer (two 12-ounce cans or bottles)
- 1 cup bottled chili sauce
- ¼ teaspoon root beer concentrate (optional)
- 6 to 8 dashes hot pepper sauce (optional)
- 8 to 10 hamburger buns or kaiser rolls, split (toasted, if you like)
- Lettuce leaves (optional)
- Tomato slices (optional)

1. Trim fat from meat. If necessary, cut roast to fit into slow cooker. Sprinkle meat with the salt and pepper. In a large skillet, brown roast on all sides in hot oil. Drain. Transfer meat to a 3½-, 4-, or 5-quart slow cooker. Add onions, the 1 cup root beer and garlic. Cover; cook on low-heat setting for 8 to 10 hours or on high-heat setting for 4 to 5 hours.

2. Meanwhile, for sauce, in a medium saucepan combine the root beer and bottled chili sauce. Bring to boiling; reduce heat.

3. Boil gently, uncovered, stirring occasionally, about 30 minutes or until mixture is reduced to 2 cups. Add root beer concentrate and bottled hot pepper sauce, if you like.

4. Transfer roast to a cutting board or serving platter. With a slotted spoon, remove onions from juices and place on serving platter. Discard juices. Using two forks, shred meat. To serve, line buns with lettuce leaves and tomato slices, if you like. Add meat and onions; spoon on sauce. **Makes 8 to 10 servings.**

Note: To store leftovers, transfer pork mixture to covered container and chill up to 24 hours. Or transfer to 1-, 2-, or 4-serving freezer containers; seal, label, and freeze up to 1 month. Thaw overnight before serving. To reheat, transfer to saucepan; cover and heat over medium-low heat until heated through, stirring occasionally. If necessary, add 2 to 4 tablespoons water to keep mixture from sticking.

Per serving: 421 cal, 9 g fat, 98 mg chol, 1,412 mg sodium, 48 g carbo, 1 g fiber, 35 g pro.

Hearty Pork and Ale Stew

PREP 30 minutes COOK 35 minutes

  2 tablespoons all-purpose flour
  ½ teaspoon crushed red pepper
  1 pound boneless pork sirloin
  2 cloves garlic, minced
  1 tablespoon cooking oil
  3 cups vegetable broth
  1 12-ounce can beer or 1½ cups vegetable
      broth
  2 large sweet potatoes, peeled and cut into
      1-inch cubes
  3 medium parsnips, peeled and sliced
      ¾ inch thick
  1 medium onion, cut into thin wedges
  2 tablespoons snipped fresh thyme or
      1½ teaspoons dried thyme, crushed
  1 tablespoon packed brown sugar
  1 tablespoon Dijon-style mustard
  4 large plum tomatoes, coarsely chopped
  2 small green apples, cored and cut into
      wedges

1. In a plastic bag, combine flour and red pepper. Trim fat from meat. Cut the meat into ¾-inch cubes. Add the meat cubes, a few at a time, to the flour mixture, shaking to coat meat.

2. In a 4-quart Dutch oven, cook meat and garlic in hot oil until the meat is browned. Stir in the vegetable broth, beer, sweet potatoes, parsnips, onion, thyme, brown sugar and mustard.

3. Bring to boiling; reduce heat. Cover and simmer for 30 minutes. Stir in tomatoes and apples. Return to boiling; reduce heat. Simmer, covered, for about 5 minutes more or until meat, vegetables and apples are tender. **Makes 6 servings.**

Per serving: 288 cal, 7 g fat, 48 mg chol, 571 mg sodium, 36 g carbo, 6 g fiber, 20 g pro.

Roasted Chicken Breasts with Caramelized Onions and Fall Fruit

PREP 30 minutes ROAST 30 minutes

  4 bone-in chicken breast halves (2 to
      2½ pounds)
  4 teaspoons chicken or turkey roasting rub
  2 large white or red onions, cut into ¾-inch
      chunks (2 cups)
  2 tablespoons butter
  2 tablespoons packed brown sugar
  1 medium Granny Smith or tart red apple,
      peeled, cored and coarsely chopped
      (1 cup)
  1 medium Bosc or Anjou pear, peeled, cored
      and coarsely chopped (1 cup)
  ⅓ cup dried cranberries, dried cherries, dried
      currants, golden raisins, snipped dried
      apricots or snipped dried figs
  2 cloves garlic, minced
  1½ teaspoons snipped fresh rosemary or
      ¾ teaspoon dried rosemary, crushed
  ½ teaspoon ground black pepper
  ¼ cup cranberry juice, apple cranberry juice,
      pear nectar, apricot nectar or dry white
      wine
  2 tablespoons dry sherry, white balsamic
      vinegar, dry vermouth or dry white wine

1. Lightly grease a shallow baking pan. Sprinkle the roasting rub onto all of the surfaces of the chicken; rub in with fingers. Place chicken, skin side up, in prepared baking pan. Roast, uncovered, in a 425° oven for 30 to 35 minutes or until chicken is no longer pink (170°).

2. Meanwhile, in a large skillet, cook onions, covered, in hot butter over medium-low heat about 15 minutes or until onions are tender, stirring occasionally. Uncover; add brown sugar. Cook and stir over medium-high heat about 5 minutes more or until onions are golden. Add apple, pear, cranberries, garlic, rosemary and pepper to skillet. Cook, covered, for 5 minutes, stirring twice. Stir in cranberry juice and dry sherry. Simmer, uncovered, for 2 to 4 minutes or until liquid is reduced by half.

3. To serve, transfer the chicken to a serving platter. Spoon caramelized onions over chicken. **Makes 4 servings.**

Per serving: 529 cal, 23 g fat, 131 mg chol, 822 mg sodium, 40 g carbo, 4 g fiber, 39 g pro.

ROASTED CHICKEN
BREASTS WITH
CARAMELIZED ONIONS
AND FALL FRUIT

The Ultimate Chicken and Noodle Casserole

Even the most health-conscious will take a day off when presented with this creamy, bubbling casserole crowned with a crispy bread crumb-nut-Parmesan topping.

PREP 35 minutes **BAKE** 30 minutes

6 ounces dried gemelli pasta (1⅔ cups) or dried medium noodles (3 cups)

2 tablespoons butter or margarine

1½ cups sliced cremini mushrooms or sliced button mushrooms

1 cup chopped onion

3 cups chopped cooked chicken*

1 15-ounce bottle mushroom Alfredo pasta sauce

1½ cups shredded Italian-blend cheeses (6 ounces)

1 9- to 10-ounce package frozen cut asparagus or frozen peas, thawed

½ cup dairy sour cream

½ cup finely chopped bottled roasted red sweet peppers

1 teaspoon dried fines herbes or Italian seasoning, crushed

½ cup panko (Japanese bread crumbs) or fine dry bread crumbs

¼ cup sliced almonds or chopped pecans, toasted

2 tablespoons grated Parmesan cheese

2 tablespoons butter, melted

1. Cook pasta according to package directions; drain. Return to pan.

2. Meanwhile, in a large saucepan, heat 2 tablespoons butter over medium heat until melted. Add mushrooms and onion; cook and stir until mushrooms are tender. Stir into pasta along with the chicken, pasta sauce, Italian-blend cheeses, asparagus, sour cream, sweet peppers and fines herbes. Transfer mixture to a 13x9x2-inch baking dish (3-quart rectangular).

3. In a small bowl, combine panko, nuts, Parmesan cheese and 2 tablespoons melted butter. Sprinkle over chicken mixture. Bake, uncovered, in a 350° oven for 30 to 35 minutes or until heated through and topping is golden. **Makes 6 servings.**

*Note: If you don't have cooked chicken on hand, pick some up at the supermarket. Look for refrigerated or frozen chopped, cooked chicken or buy a deli-roasted chicken. It will yield 1½ to 2 cups of boneless chopped meat. If you like, you can cook your own. Place 1¼ pounds of skinless, boneless chicken breasts and 2 cups water in a large skillet. Bring to boiling; reduce heat. Cover and simmer for 12 to 14 minutes or until chicken is no longer pink (170°). Drain well. Chop chicken. About 1¼ pounds of boneless breasts will give you about 3 cups cubed cooked chicken.

Per serving: 600 cal, 34 g fat, 141 mg chol, 797 mg sodium, 36 g carbo, 3 g fiber, 38 g pro.

Turkey Onion Soup

PREP 40 minutes **COOK** 1 hour

   3 medium onions, chopped (1½ cups)
   3 medium leeks, chopped (1 cup)
   1 bunch green onions, sliced (½ cup)
   3 shallots, finely chopped (⅓ cup)
   3 carrots, sliced (1½ cups)
   3 stalks celery, sliced (1½ cups)
   1 tablespoon cooking oil
   1 pound turkey breast half, skinned
5½ cups water
   ½ cup snipped fresh parsley
1½ teaspoons dried oregano, crushed
1½ teaspoons Greek seasoning
   1 teaspoon salt
   1 teaspoon fennel seeds, crushed
   ½ teaspoon freshly ground black pepper
   2 bay leaves

1. In a 4-quart Dutch oven, cook the onions, leeks, green onions, shallots, carrots and celery in hot oil over medium-high heat for 7 to 10 minutes or until tender. Add the turkey breast half, the water, ¼ cup of the parsley, the oregano, Greek seasoning, salt, fennel seeds, pepper and bay leaves. Bring to boiling; reduce heat. Cover and simmer for 1 to 2 hours or until turkey breast is tender.

2. Remove turkey from Dutch oven. Cut meat from bones; discard bones. Chop meat and return to Dutch oven. Remove bay leaves. **Makes 6 servings.**

Per serving: 227 cal, 5 g fat, 80 mg chol, 516 mg sodium, 13 g carbo, 3 g fiber, 33 g pro.

Angel Chicken

PREP 15 minutes **COOK** 4 to 5 hours on low

   4 skinless, boneless chicken breast halves
      (about 1½ pounds)
   1 tablespoon vegetable oil (optional)
   1 8-ounce package fresh button
      mushrooms, quartered
   1 8-ounce package fresh shiitake
      mushrooms, stems removed, caps sliced
   ¼ cup butter
   1 0.7-ounce package Italian dry salad
      dressing mix
   1 10¾-ounce can condensed golden
      mushroom soup
   ½ cup dry white wine
   ½ of a 8-ounce tub cream cheese spread
      with chives and onion
      Hot cooked rice or angel hair pasta
      Snipped fresh chives or sliced green
      onions (optional)

1. If you like, brown chicken on both sides in a large skillet in hot oil over medium heat. Combine mushrooms in a 3½- or 4-quart slow cooker; top with chicken. Melt butter in a medium saucepan; stir in Italian dressing mix. Stir in mushroom soup, white wine and cream cheese until melted; pour over chicken.

2. Cover; cook on low-heat setting for 4 to 5 hours.

3. Serve chicken and sauce over cooked rice. Sprinkle with chives, if you like. **Makes 4 servings.**

Per serving: 602 cal, 25 g fat, 162 mg chol, 1,944 mg sodium, 41 g carbo, 2 g fiber, 47 g pro.

ANGEL CHICKEN

Venison Sausage Focaccia

It's not uncommon for deer hunters to make their own venison sausage. If you can't find venison sausage, use regular sweet Italian sausage.

START TO FINISH 30 minutes

1 medium onion, cut into ½-inch-thick slices
⅓ cup bottled clear Italian salad dressing
2 red and/or yellow sweet peppers
1 pound uncooked venison sweet Italian sausage links or sweet Italian sausage links (4 to 5 links)
⅓ cup mayonnaise or salad dressing
1 tablespoon Dijon-style mustard
1 9-inch desired-flavor focaccia bread, halved horizontally

1. Brush onion slices with some of the dressing; set aside. Cut tops off peppers and discard. Remove seeds and membranes from peppers. Cut peppers crosswise into ¼-inch thick slices. Toss pepper slices with remaining salad dressing in a large bowl.

2. For a charcoal grill, arrange medium-hot coals around a drip pan. Test for medium heat over drip pan. Prick sausage links with a fork in several places. Place sausages on grill rack over drip pan and onion slices directly over the coals around edge of grill rack. Cover and grill 10 minutes. Turn sausage and onion slices. Place pepper slices on grill rack directly over the coals. Cover and grill 5 to 15 minutes more, turning peppers once and removing vegetables from the grill when they are crisp-tender. Cook sausages until the internal temperature registers 160° when tested with an instant read thermometer. (For a gas grill, preheat grill. Reduce heat to medium high. Add vegetables and sausage to grill as above. Cover and grill as above.) Remove sausages from grill.

3. Meanwhile, combine mayonnaise and mustard; spread on cut sides of focaccia. Bias-slice sausage ¼ inch thick. Separate onion slices into rings, if necessary. Arrange sausage, peppers and onions on focaccia bottom. Add focaccia top. Press down gently on focaccia top to slightly compress sandwich. Cut into wedges to serve. **Makes 6 servings.**

Per serving: 346 cal, 21 g fat, 74 mg chol, 758 mg sodium, 10 g carbo, 1 g fiber, 19 g pro.

Sandwiches of all kinds make perfect tailgating fare. Do your chopping and as much prepping as possible at home, transporting cut-up veggies in resealable plastic bags in the cooler. When you get to your tailgating site, all you have to do is set up the grill and get cooking.

Cider-Brined Coho Salmon with Dijon Cream

A cider-tarragon marinade infuses this freshwater fish with flavor. Before serving, the fish is draped with an elegant cream sauce scented with aniselike tarragon.

PREP 25 minutes **MARINATE** 4 hours **BROIL** 5 minutes

1 1-pound fresh salmon fillet
1 cup cold water
1 cup apple cider
2 tablespoons kosher salt
¼ cup snipped fresh tarragon
½ teaspoon ground black pepper
  Nonstick cooking spray
1 tablespoon olive oil
1 tablespoon butter
1 large shallot, finely chopped
1 tablespoon all-purpose flour
½ cup dry white wine
½ cup whipping cream
2 teaspoons Dijon-style mustard
½ teaspoon salt
  Fresh tarragon sprigs (optional)

1. Rinse salmon; pat dry with paper towels. Place salmon in a large resealable plastic bag set in a shallow dish. For marinade: In a medium bowl, stir together the water, cider and kosher salt until salt dissolves. Stir in snipped tarragon and pepper. Pour over salmon; seal bag. Marinate in the refrigerator for 4 hours, turning bag occasionally.

2. Preheat broiler. Line a baking sheet with foil; lightly coat foil with nonstick cooking spray. Drain salmon, discarding marinade. Pat salmon dry with paper towels. Discard brine. Place salmon, skin side down, on prepared baking sheet. Brush salmon with olive oil. Broil 5 to 6 inches from the heat for 5 to 7 minutes or until fish flakes when tested with a fork. Remove from broiler; and cover with foil to keep warm.

3. In a small saucepan, melt butter over medium heat. Add shallot; cook and stir for 4 to 5 minutes or until tender. Stir in flour. Cook and stir for 1 minute. Add wine, cream, mustard and ½ teaspoon salt, whisking until smooth. Cook and stir until thickened and bubbly; cook and stir 1 minute more. Remove from heat. Place salmon on a serving platter. Drizzle with sauce. If you like, garnish with tarragon sprigs. **Makes 4 servings.**

Per serving: 379 cal, 26 g fat, 107 mg chol, 619 mg sodium, 4 g carbo, 0 g fiber, 25 g pro.

The lakes and streams of the Midwest bear a bounty of freshwater fish—trout, Coho salmon, whitefish and walleye among them.

Rigatoni with Spinach, Walnuts, Sweet Potatoes and Goat Cheese

START TO FINISH 30 minutes

- 12 ounces dried rigatoni pasta
- 2 tablespoons butter
- 2 tablespoons extra virgin olive oil
- 1 large sweet potato, peeled and cut into ¾-inch pieces (12 ounces)
- ½ of a medium red onion, thinly sliced
- 4 cups fresh baby spinach leaves
- 4 ounces semisoft goat cheese (chèvre) or feta cheese, crumbled
- ½ cup coarsely chopped walnuts, toasted
- ¼ cup loosely packed fresh basil leaves, torn
- 2 tablespoons extra virgin olive oil
  Salt or kosher salt
  Ground black pepper
  Italian bread (optional)

1. In a 5- to 6-quart Dutch oven, cook pasta according to package directions; drain. Return pasta to pan; keep warm.

2. Meanwhile, in a large skillet, melt butter and heat 2 tablespoons olive oil over medium-high heat. Add the sweet potato. Cook for 8 minutes or until nearly tender, gently stirring occasionally. Add the onion; cook about 5 minutes more or until potato and onion are tender and lightly browned, gently stirring occasionally.

3. Add spinach to potato mixture, tossing gently just until spinach is wilted. Add potato mixture to pasta along with goat cheese, walnuts, basil and 2 tablespoons olive oil. Toss gently to combine. Season to taste with salt and black pepper. Serve immediately with Italian bread, if you like. **Makes 6 servings.**

Per serving: 490 cal, 26 g fat, 25 mg chol, 354 mg sodium, 52 g carbo, 4 g fiber, 14 g pro.

Butternut Squash Risotto with Honeycrisp Apples

PREP 20 minutes   **COOK** 20 minutes

- ¼ cup chopped onion
- 4 cloves garlic, minced
- 2 tablespoons unsalted butter
- ⅔ cup arborio rice
- 1 14-ounce can vegetable broth
- ¼ cup water
- ½ cup dry white wine
- ¼ cup peeled and finely chopped butternut squash
- 2 tablespoons peeled and finely chopped sweet crisp apple (such as Honeycrisp or Pink Lady)
- 2 slices crisp-cooked applewood smoked bacon, crumbled
- ½ cup baby spinach leaves
- 2 tablespoons unsalted butter, softened
- 2 tablespoons grated Parmesan cheese
- 2 tablespoons snipped fresh chives
- 2 tablespoons whipping cream
  Kosher salt or salt
  Freshly ground black pepper

1. In medium saucepan, cook onion and garlic in 2 tablespoons hot butter over medium heat for 3 to 4 minutes until onion is tender; add rice. Cook and stir over medium heat about 5 minutes more or until rice is lightly golden.

2. Meanwhile, in a small saucepan, bring broth and the water to boiling; reduce heat and simmer.

3. Carefully stir the wine into the rice mixture. Cook and stir until all liquid is absorbed. Slowly add ½ cup of the broth mixture to the rice mixture, stirring constantly. Continue to cook and stir over medium heat until liquid is absorbed. Add another ½ cup of the broth mixture. Continue to cook and stir over medium heat until liquid is absorbed.

4. Stir in squash, apples and bacon. Slowly add another ½ cup of the broth mixture to the rice mixture, stirring constantly. Continue to cook and stir over medium heat until liquid is absorbed. Add remaining broth mixture. Cook and stir until the rice is slightly creamy and just tender (al dente).

5. Fold in the spinach, 2 tablespoons softened butter, Parmesan cheese, chives and whipping cream; heat through. Season to taste with salt and black pepper. **Makes 2½ cups (4 side-dish servings).**

Per serving: 280 cal, 17 g fat, 47 mg chol, 590 mg sodium, 23 g carbo, 1 g fiber, 5 g pro.

The country's favorite fruit is grown in abundance in the Midwest. Early fall is the perfect time to visit a pick-your-own orchard or farm stand.

Shaved Vegetable Salad with Brown Butter Vinaigrette

It may look and sound complicated, but this recipe is the essence of simplicity. It showcases fall produce at the peak of perfection, beautifully prepared and tossed with a velvety, nutty-flavor brown butter vinaigrette.

START TO FINISH 50 minutes

Brown Butter Vinaigrette (recipe follows)
¼ cup dried currants, raisins or dried cranberries
1 pound Brussels sprouts
1 large fennel bulb
1 medium shallot
½ cup slivered almonds, toasted
1 tablespoon snipped fresh dill
¼ cup shaved Parmesan or Parmigiano-Reggiano cheese
Olive oil (optional)

1. Prepare Brown Butter Vinaigrette; set aside and keep warm while preparing the salad. In a small bowl, soak currants in warm water to cover; set aside.

2. Trim stems and remove any wilted outer leaves from the Brussels sprouts; wash and drain. Slice thinly using a food processor or sharp knife. Place in a large bowl.

3. Cut off and discard fennel stalks. Remove any wilted outer layers and cut a thin slice from the base of fennel bulb; wash and drain. Stand fennel bulb upright on cutting board; cut into quarters. Cut out the core; discard. Thinly slice the fennel with food processor or sharp knife; transfer to bowl with Brussels sprouts. Thinly slice shallot with food processor or sharp knife; add to sprouts.

4. Drain the currants and add to the vegetable mixture along with the almonds and dill. Add the Brown Butter Vinaigrette; toss to coat the salad well.

5. To serve, use tongs to place mounds of the salad on salad plates. Garnish with shaved Parmesan and, if you like, a little olive oil. **Makes 6 side-dish servings.**

Brown Butter Vinaigrette: Fill a large bowl half full with cold water; set aside. In a heavy medium saucepan, melt 1 cup unsalted butter (do not stir) over medium-high heat until it starts to take on an amber color (about 6 minutes); reduce heat to medium. Slowly and carefully swirl the pan until amber color of the butter changes to deep amber with burnt specks at the bottom of the pan and the foaming decreases (about 2 minutes). (Butter will have a pleasant nutty aroma.) Remove saucepan from heat and dip the bottom into the cold water to stop the cooking. Set butter aside to cool slightly. Whisk ¼ cup champagne vinegar, ¼ cup olive oil, 2 tablespoons lemon juice and 1 teaspoon kosher salt into the warm butter until well combined. Makes about 1¼ cups.

Per serving: 482 cal, 45 g fat, 84 mg chol, 430 mg sodium, 18 g carbo, 6 g fiber, 7 g pro.

In some of the smallest towns and rural areas of the Midwest, travelers come upon culinary surprises. This recipe comes from the homegrown-goes-uptown menu of the Joseph Decuis restaurant in tiny (1,500 souls) Roanoke, Indiana.

WHEAT BERRY WALDORF SALAD

Wheat Berry Waldorf Salad

PREP 30 minutes **COOK** 30 minutes **CHILL** 6 to 24 hours plus up to 4 hours

2½ cups water
¾ cup wheat berries, rinsed
⅓ cup olive oil
¼ cup snipped fresh Italian (flat-leaf) parsley
¼ cup cider vinegar or rice vinegar
¼ cup apple juice, apple cider or lemon juice
1 to 2 tablespoons sugar
1 teaspoon salt
½ teaspoon ground cinnamon or
 ¼ teaspoon ground nutmeg
1 large Granny Smith apple, unpeeled, cored and chopped (1½ cups)
1 large Braeburn, Jonagold or Rome Beauty apple, unpeeled, cored and chopped (1¼ cups)
½ cup finely chopped celery
½ cup dried cranberries, dried tart cherries and/or golden raisins
½ cup seedless green and/or red grapes, halved
6 to 8 Bibb or Boston lettuce leaves
 Honey-roasted sliced almonds or honey-roasted peanuts

1. In a small bowl, combine the water and wheat berries. Cover and chill in the refrigerator for 6 to 24 hours. Do not drain; transfer to a medium saucepan. Bring to boiling; reduce heat. Simmer, covered, about 30 minutes or until tender with a firm, chewy texture. Drain; transfer to bowl to cool.

2. In a screw-top jar, combine oil, parsley, vinegar, apple juice, sugar, salt and cinnamon. Cover and shake well to combine. Drizzle dressing over warm wheat berries; stir to coat. Set aside.

3. In a large bowl, combine apples, celery, cranberries and grapes. Stir in wheat berry mixture; mix well. Cover and chill in the refrigerator for up to 4 hours if not serving immediately.

4. To serve, arrange lettuce cups on a large platter or divide them among individual salad plates. Spoon salad into the lettuce. Sprinkle with nuts. **Makes 6 to 8 side-dish servings.**

Per serving: 321 cal, 16 g fat, 0 mg chol, 409 mg sodium, 45 g carbo, 7 g fiber, 5 g pro.

Praline Sweet Potatoes

PREP 25 minutes **BAKE** 30 minutes

4 medium sweet potatoes or yams (1½ pounds)
½ to ¾ cup granulated sugar
¼ cup butter, melted
¼ teaspoon salt
½ cup evaporated milk
2 beaten eggs
¼ cup packed brown sugar
2 tablespoons all-purpose flour
1 tablespoon butter, melted and cooled slightly
¼ cup chopped pecans

1. Wash and peel potatoes; cut into quarters. Cook in enough boiling, lightly salted water to cover for 25 to 30 minutes or until tender; drain well.

2. Grease a 8x8x2-inch baking dish. In a large mixing bowl, beat sweet potatoes with an electric mixer on low speed until smooth. Beat in the sugar, the ¼ cup melted butter and salt until well combined. Add milk and eggs. Beat just until combined. Spread in baking dish.

3. In a small mixing bowl, combine brown sugar, flour and 1 tablespoon melted butter. Stir in pecans. Sprinkle topping over the potato mixture. Bake in a 350° oven for 30 minutes or until set. **Makes 6 servings.**

Per serving: 365 cal, 17 g fat, 104 mg chol, 257 mg sodium, 50 g carbo, 3 g fiber, 6 g pro.

Calabaza Squash Gratin with Goat Cheese, Sage and Hazelnuts

Calabaza squash has a butternut-like flavor and firm texture. It's lovely in this elegant gratin, but for a simpler preparation, just bake it, cut in chunks and tossed with butter and herbs.

PREP 40 minutes **ROAST** 25 minutes **BAKE** 35 minutes **STAND** 5 minutes

- 1 3¼-pound calabaza or butternut squash or pie pumpkin, peeled, seeded and cut into 1-inch cubes (about 8 cups)
- 2 tablespoons olive oil
- 1½ teaspoons kosher salt
- ½ teaspoon freshly ground black pepper
- ¼ cup unsalted butter
- 2 cups thinly sliced leeks* (6 medium leeks)
- 2 teaspoons snipped fresh sage or ½ teaspoon dried sage, crushed
- 6 ounces soft chèvre (goat cheese), crumbled, or cream cheese, cut into ½-inch cubes
- 1 cup whipping cream or heavy cream
- ½ cup hazelnuts (filberts) or pumpkin seeds, coarsely chopped

1. Place squash in a shallow roasting pan. Drizzle with oil and sprinkle with 1 teaspoon of the salt and the pepper; toss to coat. Roast in a 400° oven about 25 minutes or until tender, stirring once. Set aside. Reduce oven temperature to 375°.

2. Meanwhile, in a large saucepan or skillet, melt 3 tablespoons of the butter over medium heat. Add leeks and sage to saucepan and cook for 4 to 5 minutes or until leeks are tender but not brown, stirring frequently. Remove from heat; set aside.

3. Butter a 2-quart rectangular baking dish with the remaining 1 tablespoon butter. Spread half of the leek mixture over the bottom of the buttered baking dish; add half of the squash and dot with half of the goat cheese. Repeat the layers with the remaining leeks, squash and cheese.

4. Pour whipping cream evenly over the squash layers. Sprinkle with remaining ½ teaspoon salt and the hazelnuts. Bake, uncovered, in a 375° oven about 35 minutes or until the cream is bubbly and the nuts are toasted. Let stand for 5 minutes before serving. **Makes 8 to 10 servings.**

Per serving: 352 cal, 30 g fat, 66 mg chol, 460 mg sodium, 16 g carbo, 3 g fiber, 7 g pro.

*Note: To prepare leeks, remove green portions. Halve leeks lengthwise. Wash thoroughly; pat dry with paper towels. Trim root from base; cut into slices.

Eye-catching gourds and squash—solid color or striated, fat or slender, round or oblong — announce in no uncertain terms that fall has arrived.

Crumb-Topped Apple Trio Pie

A blend of sweet and tart apples—Granny Smith, Jonagold and Braeburn—mixes it up in this easy fruit pie.

PREP 40 minutes **BAKE** 1 hour 5 minutes **COOL** 1 hour

½ of a 15-ounce package rolled refrigerated unbaked piecrust (1 crust)

2 teaspoons butter, melted

2 cups peeled, cored and thinly sliced Granny Smith apples (about ¾ pound)

2 cups peeled, cored and thinly sliced Jonagold or Jonathan apples (about ¾ pound)

2 cups peeled, cored and thinly sliced Braeburn, McIntosh or Northern Spy apples (about ¾ pound)

⅔ cup sugar

2 tablespoons all-purpose flour

2 to 3 teaspoons ground cinnamon

½ teaspoon salt

Walnut Crumb Topping (recipe follows)

Vanilla Ice Cream

1. Let piecrust stand according to package directions. Unroll piecrust; place into a 9-inch pie plate. Tuck piecrust under and flute edges. Do not prick piecrust. Brush the piecrust bottom and sides with the melted butter; set aside.

2. In a large bowl, combine the apples. In a small bowl, stir together sugar, flour, cinnamon and salt. Sprinkle sugar mixture over the fruit. Toss to combine. Let stand for 10 minutes. Transfer apple filling to pastry-lined pie plate. Mound the Walnut Crumb Topping over filling.

3. To prevent overbrowning, cover edge of pie with foil. Place the pie on the center rack of a 375° oven. Place a large baking sheet covered with foil on a rack under the pie. Bake for 30 minutes. Remove foil. Bake for 35 to 40 minutes more or until apples are tender, filling is bubbly and topping is golden. (If necessary, loosely cover top of pie with foil the last 30 to 40 minutes.) Cool 1 hour on a wire rack. Serve pie slightly warm with ice cream. **Makes 8 servings.**

Walnut Crumb Topping: In a food processor, combine ¾ cup walnuts, ¼ cup granulated sugar and ¼ cup packed brown sugar. Cover and process to grind the walnuts. Remove the lid; add ½ cup all-purpose flour, ½ cup rolled oats, ¼ teaspoon salt and ¼ teaspoon ground cinnamon. Cover and process until combined. Remove the lid; scatter 6 tablespoons cold butter, cut into ¼-inch-thick slices, over the flour mixture. Cover and process until mixture resembles coarse crumbs. Transfer to a large bowl; rub the crumbs between your fingers to make large, buttery crumbs.

Per serving: 654 cal, 32 g fat, 60 mg chol, 455 mg sodium, 86 g carbo, 4 g fiber, 8 g pro.

Pumpkin-Apple Butter Pie

The two most quintessential fruits of fall—pumpkin and apple—pair up in this custardy pie. The nut-studded crust can be made with either pecans or walnuts.

PREP 30 minutes **BAKE** 55 minutes

Nut Pastry (recipe follows)
1 egg, slightly beaten
1 tablespoon water
Granulated sugar (optional)
1 15-ounce can pumpkin
½ cup packed brown sugar
½ cup apple butter
1 teaspoon ground cinnamon
½ teaspoon ground ginger
¼ teaspoon salt
⅛ teaspoon ground cloves
2 eggs, slightly beaten
1 egg yolk, slightly beaten
½ cup whipping cream
½ cup chopped pecans or walnuts
2 tablespoons butter, softened
2 tablespoons all-purpose flour
2 tablespoons packed brown sugar
Sweetened whipped cream (optional)

1. Prepare the Nut Pastry. On a lightly floured surface, roll out half of the pastry to fit a 9-inch pie plate. Ease into pie plate; trim pastry to edge of pie plate. Roll out remaining pastry to ⅛-inch thickness. Cut out ½- to 1-inch fall or holiday designs. In a small bowl, combine the one egg and the water. Brush over edge of pastry in pie plate. Arrange cutouts around edge of pastry. Brush cutouts with egg mixture. Sprinkle with granulated sugar, if you like. Set pie plate aside.

2. In a medium bowl, combine pumpkin, ½ cup brown sugar, apple butter, cinnamon, ginger, salt and cloves. Add two eggs and egg yolk; beat lightly with a fork just until combined. Gradually add whipping cream; stir until combined. Turn into prepared crust.

3. Loosely cover edge of pastry with foil to prevent overbrowning. Bake in a 375° oven for 20 minutes. Remove foil; bake 20 minutes more. Meanwhile, in a small bowl, combine the nuts, butter, flour and 2 tablespoons brown sugar. Sprinkle over the pie. Bake for 15 to 20 minutes more or until a knife inserted near the center comes out clean.

4. Cool on wire rack. Cover and chill in the refrigerator within 2 hours. Serve with whipped cream, if you like. **Makes 8 to 10 servings.**

Nut Pastry: In a medium bowl, stir together 2¼ cups all-purpose flour and ¾ teaspoon salt. Using a pastry blender, cut in ⅔ cup shortening until pieces are pea-size. Stir in ½ cup ground pecans or walnuts. Sprinkle 8 to 10 tablespoon water, 1 tablespoon at a time, over mixture and toss until moistened. Form into a ball.

Per serving: 665 cal, 37 g fat, 135 mg chol, 365 mg sodium, 75 g carbo, 5 g fiber, 9 g pro.

Pumpkin-Praline Layer Cake

A gooey pecan glaze gives this super-moist pumpkin spice cake a glossy look and fabulous flavor. Substitute regular walnut extract for the black walnut flavoring, if you like—or leave it out altogether.

PREP 20 minutes **BAKE** 35 minutes **COOL** 5 minutes

1 cup packed brown sugar
½ cup butter or margarine
¼ cup whipping cream
¾ cup chopped pecans
2 cups all-purpose flour
2 teaspoons baking powder
2 teaspoons pumpkin pie spice
1 teaspoon baking soda
1 teaspoon salt
1⅔ cups granulated sugar
1 cup cooking oil
4 eggs
2 cups canned pumpkin
¼ teaspoon black walnut flavoring (optional)
    Whipped Cream Topping (recipe follows)

1. In a heavy saucepan, combine brown sugar, butter and whipping cream. Cook over low heat until the brown sugar just dissolves, stirring occasionally. Pour mixture into two 9x1½-inch round baking pans. Sprinkle evenly with the pecans. Let the mixture cool slightly.

2. In a bowl, stir together the flour, baking powder, pumpkin pie spice, baking soda and salt. Set it aside.

3. In a large mixing bowl, beat together the granulated sugar, cooking oil and eggs. Add the pumpkin and dry ingredients alternately to the oil mixture, beating just until the mixture is combined. Stir in the black walnut flavoring, if you like.

4. Carefully spoon the batter over the pecan-brown sugar mixture in the baking pans. Place pans on a baking sheet. Bake in a 350° oven for 35 to 40 minutes or until toothpicks inserted in the centers come out clean. Cool the cakes in pans on wire racks for 5 minutes. Invert them onto wire racks, replacing any brown sugar mixture that remains in the pans. Cool before assembling.*

5. Meanwhile, prepare the Whipped Cream Topping.

6. To assemble the cake, place one cake layer on a serving plate, praline side up. Spread with the topping. Add the second layer, praline side up. Pipe or dollop with the remaining topping. Sprinkle lightly with some additional pie spice, if you like. **Makes 12 servings.**

Whipped Cream Topping: In a clean mixing bowl, beat 1¾ cups whipping cream with an electric mixer until soft peaks form (tips curl). Add ¼ cup powdered sugar and ¼ teaspoon vanilla. Beat the topping mixture until stiff peaks form (the tips stand straight).

*Note: Plan to assemble this cake no more than 1½ hours before serving, so the whipped cream doesn't break down. Keep the cake chilled until it's served.

Per serving: 704 cal, 47 g fat, 146 mg chol, 466 mg sodium, 69 g carbo, 2 g fiber

Special occasions call for spectacular desserts, and this glazed and layered beauty certainly qualifies.

Spiced Pear-Cranberry Cobbler

The sweetness of the pears beautifully complements the pleasant tartness of the cranberries in this warm fruit dessert topped with pumpkin-cornmeal biscuits.

PREP 40 minutes **BAKE** 1 hour **COOL** 30 minutes

- 6 medium Bosc, Anjou and/or Asian pears, peeled, cored and coarsely chopped (6 cups)
- 1 16-ounce can whole cranberry sauce
- 1 cup fresh cranberries or ⅓ cup dried cranberries or dried cherries
- ½ cup packed brown sugar
- 1 teaspoon pumpkin pie spice or ground cinnamon
- ¾ cup all-purpose flour
- ¼ cup cornmeal
- 3 tablespoons granulated sugar
- 1½ teaspoons baking powder
- ½ teaspoon pumpkin pie spice or ground cinnamon
- ¼ cup cold butter, cut up
- 1 egg, lightly beaten
- ½ cup canned pumpkin
- 2 tablespoons half-and-half, light cream, milk or pear nectar
  Whipping cream, half-and-half, light cream or vanilla ice cream

1. In a large bowl, combine pears, cranberry sauce, cranberries, brown sugar and the 1 teaspoon pumpkin pie spice. Transfer filling to a 2- or 2½-quart casserole. Bake, covered, in a 375° oven for 30 minutes.

2. Meanwhile, for biscuit topping, in a medium bowl, combine flour, cornmeal, the 3 tablespoons granulated sugar, baking powder and the ½ teaspoon pumpkin pie spice. Using a pastry blender, cut butter into flour mixture until pieces are pea-size. In a small bowl, combine egg, pumpkin and half-and-half. Add pumpkin mixture to flour mixture all at once, stirring until just combined.

3. Remove casserole dish from oven. Spoon the topping into eight mounds on top of the hot pear mixture. If you like, sprinkle with a little additional granulated sugar or coarse sugar.

4. Bake, uncovered, about 30 minutes more or until a wooden toothpick inserted near the center of the biscuit topping comes out clean. Cool for 30 minutes. Serve warm with whipping cream. **Makes 8 servings.**

Per serving: 417 cal, 13 g fat, 64 mg chol, 148 mg sodium, 76 g carbo, 6 g fiber, 4 g pro.

The cranberry bogs of Wisconsin produce more of this tart and tangy fruit than any other state in the country. In fact, it is the state's No.1 fruit crop.

Indulgent Caramel Apples

Coat your caramel apples choosing toppings from our list below. Good news—the caramel coating we created doesn't stick to your teeth!

PREP 30 minutes **STAND** 25 minutes **CHILL** 30 minutes

- 6 to 8 small red and/or green tart apples (such as Granny Smith, Macintosh or Jonathan*)
- 6 to 8 wooden crafts or popsicle sticks
- 2 cups assorted toppings (such as coarsely chopped mixed nuts, pistachios, peanuts, almonds or cashews; coconut, toasted; candy-coated milk chocolate pieces; candy-coated peanut butter-flavor pieces; miniature semisweet chocolate pieces; tiny marshmallows; ready-to-eat sweetened cereal; granola; dried fruit bits; shelled pumpkin seeds; toffee bits; cocoa nibs; and/or decorative sprinkles)
- 1 14-ounce package vanilla caramels, unwrapped
- 2 tablespoons whipping cream, half-and-half or light cream
- ⅔ cup semisweet or bittersweet chocolate pieces (3 ounces)
- 2 teaspoons shortening
- ⅔ cup milk chocolate pieces (3 ounces)
- 2 teaspoons shortening
- ⅔ cup white baking pieces (3 ounces)
- 2 teaspoons shortening

1. Line a large baking sheet with foil; coat foil with nonstick cooking spray. Set aside.

2. Wash apples; pat dry. Remove stems. Insert wooden sticks into stem end of each apple; set aside. Place apples on prepared baking sheet. Place assorted toppings in separate shallow dishes or pie plates.

3. In a medium saucepan, combine caramels and whipping cream. Cook and stir over medium-low heat until caramels are completely melted, stirring constantly. Turn heat to low. Working quickly, dip the bottom half of each apple into hot caramel mixture; turn to coat. Allow excess caramel mixture to drip off. (Heat caramel again over low heat if it becomes too thick to easily coat apples.)

4. Immediately dip bottoms of apples in assorted toppings, sprinkling some toppings onto sides of apples. Place apples, coated sides down, on prepared baking sheet. Let stand about 25 minutes or until set.

5. In a small saucepan, stir semisweet chocolate pieces and the 2 teaspoons shortening over low heat until melted. Transfer to a small resealable plastic bag. Seal and snip off a tiny corner. Drizzle by zigzagging the chocolate over stem end of apples allowing excess chocolate to drip down sides of apples. Chill 10 minutes to set.

6. In a small saucepan, stir milk chocolate pieces and the 2 teaspoons shortening over low heat until melted. Drizzle over apples as directed above. Chill 10 minutes to set.

7. In a small saucepan, stir white chocolate pieces and the 2 teaspoons shortening over low heat until melted. Drizzle over apples as directed above. Chill 10 minutes to set. Store in the refrigerator for 2 to 3 days. **Makes 6 to 8 servings.**

Per serving: 90 cal, 58 g fat, 12 mg chol, 424 mg sodium, 109 g carbo, 8 g fiber, 13 g pro.

*Note: Apples may have a waxy coating on them that keeps the caramel from sticking. Dipping apples in boiling water for about 10 seconds will melt that waxy residue so the caramel will stick to the apple. After dipping in the water, wipe dry with a paper towel.

WARM-ME-UP CHICKEN
CHILI, PAGE 210

Winter

APPETIZERS

Cranberry-Sauced Meatballs 192

Festive Cranberry Brie 195

Hot Artichoke and Roasted Pepper Asiago Cheese Dip 192

Pear-Shape Sake Cheese Ball 195

Stuffed Party Pinwheels 197

Swiss-Artichoke Dip 192

BREAKFAST

Gingerbread Pancakes 182

Herbed Egg-Potato Bake 185

Stuffed Croissant Breakfast Strata 185

BREADS

Chocolate-Nut Cinnamon Rolls 191

Cranberry Scones 188

English Muffins in a Loaf with Honey Butter 188

Jumbo Coffee Cake Muffins 186

Sour Cream-Cranberry Muffins 186

BEVERAGES

Hot Buttered Rum 197

Old Blue Eyes Martini 198

Punch with a Punch 198

Seduction Martini 198

Spiced Pear Tea 197

MAIN DISHES

Beef Short Ribs Over Gorgonzola Polenta 202

Cheesy Potato Soup 207

Fireside Beef Stew with Root Vegetables 204

Roast Breast of Chicken with Mushroom and Wild Rice Stuffing 205

Southwestern Potato-Sausage Chowder 207

Warm-Me-Up Chicken Chili 210

Wild Rice and Chicken Soup 207

Wine-Marinated Pot Roast 201

Zippy Holiday Pork Roast 205

SIDES

Champagne-Poached Pear Salad 213

Cranberry-Apple Corn Bread Stuffing 217

Holiday Cauliflower 214

Roasted Root Vegetables 214

Wilted Spinach Salad with Hot Bacon Dressing 213

SWEETS

Almond Toffee 230

Black-Bottom Pecan Pie 220

Chocolate- Caramel Fondue 230

Chocolate Chip Bread Pudding 230

Coconut Balls 224

Fanciful Peppermint Fudge 228

Old-Fashioned Buttermilk-Coconut Pie 220

Orange-Ginger Cookie Sandwiches 226

Pecan Butter Balls 228

Sparkling Sour Cream Sugar Cookies 224

Very Ginger Pound Cake 223

Gingerbread Pancakes

They may taste like dessert, but these buttermilk hotcakes made with whole wheat flour and flavored with molasses and gingerbread spices make a wholesome breakfast.

PREP 20 minutes **COOK** 4 minutes per batch

1¾ cups all-purpose flour
½ cup whole wheat flour
¼ cup packed brown sugar
2 teaspoons baking powder
1 teaspoon ground ginger
1 teaspoon ground cinnamon
½ teaspoon baking soda
½ teaspoon salt
¼ teaspoon ground nutmeg or
    ⅛ teaspoon ground cloves
2 eggs, lightly beaten
1½ cups buttermilk
⅓ cup mild-flavor molasses
3 tablespoons vegetable oil
    Butter (optional)
    Pure maple syrup
1 medium Gala, Fuji or Golden Delicious
    apple, cored and sliced crosswise into
    paper-thin slices

1. In a large bowl, combine all-purpose flour, whole wheat flour, brown sugar, baking powder, ginger, cinnamon, baking soda, salt and nutmeg. Make a well in the center of the flour mixture.

2. In a medium bowl, whisk together eggs, buttermilk, molasses and oil. Add milk mixture all at once to flour mixture. Stir just until moistened (batter should be slightly lumpy).

3. Heat a lightly greased griddle or heavy skillet over medium heat. For standard-size pancakes, spoon about ¼ cup batter onto hot griddle. Spread batter, if necessary. For dollar-size pancakes, use about 2 tablespoons batter. Cook over medium heat about 2 minutes on each side or until pancakes are golden brown. Turn over when pancake surfaces are bubbly and edges are slightly dry.

4. Serve immediately. (Or keep warm in a loosely covered ovenproof dish in a 200° oven.) If you like, top pancakes with butter. Serve with warm maple syrup. Garnish with apple slices. **Makes 16 standard-size pancakes or 32 mini pancakes.**

Per standard-size pancake: 247 cal, 4 g fat, 27 mg chol, 198 mg sodium, 51 g carbo, 1 g fiber, 4 g pro.

After a hearty breakfast, a crisp winter walk invigorates. If you're lucky, you may see something spectacular, like eagles soaring over the Mississippi River town of Clarksville, Missouri.

STUFFED CROISSANT
BREAKFAST STRATA

Stuffed Croissant Breakfast Strata

Using croissants rather than standard bread in this make-ahead strata layered with bacon, vegetables and cheese dresses it up just a bit.

BROIL 1 minute **PREP** 25 minutes
COOK 10 minutes **CHILL** 8 to 24 hours
BAKE 50 minutes **STAND** 40 minutes

    6 to 7 purchased croissants
    8 slices bacon
    1 cup chopped onion
    1 cup chopped red and/or green sweet
        peppers or sliced, halved zucchini
    1 cup sliced fresh cremini mushrooms
    1½ teaspoons dried basil, oregano or thyme,
        crushed
    2 cups lightly packed, coarsely chopped
        fresh spinach
    8 ounces colby and Monterey Jack cheese
        or American cheese, shredded (2 cups)
    6 eggs
    2 cups milk
    3 tablespoons Dijon-style mustard
    ½ teaspoon ground black pepper

1. Preheat the broiler. Slice the croissants in half horizontally. Arrange croissant halves, cut sides up, in a single layer on an extra-large baking sheet. Broil 4 to 5 inches from the heat for 1 to 2 minutes or until light brown. Set aside.

2. In a very large skillet, cook bacon over medium heat until crisp. Drain bacon on paper towels, reserving 1 tablespoon drippings in skillet. Crumble bacon; set aside.

3. Cook onion, sweet peppers, mushrooms and basil in hot bacon drippings about 5 minutes or until vegetables are almost tender, stirring occasionally. Add spinach; stir until wilted and well coated. Transfer onion mixture to a colander set in sink; drain. Stir in bacon. Set aside.

4. In a greased 3-quart rectangular baking dish, arrange croissant bottoms, cut sides up, in a single layer, overlapping slightly. Sprinkle cheese over croissants. Spoon onion mixture over cheese; add croissant tops, cut sides down.

5. In a large bowl, beat eggs with a rotary beater; beat in milk, mustard and black pepper. Carefully pour egg mixture over layers; gently press down on croissants. Cover and chill in the refrigerator for 8 to 24 hours.

6. Uncover strata. Let stand at room temperature for 30 minutes. Bake, uncovered, in a 325° oven for 50 to 55 minutes or until a knife inserted near the center comes out clean and strata puffs up, covering with foil the last 15 minutes of baking time to avoid overbrowning. Remove from oven. Let stand for 10 minutes before serving. Serve warm. **Makes 10 to 12 servings.**

Per serving: 361 cal, 23 g fat, 182 mg chol, 735 mg sodium, 22 g carbo, 2 g fiber, 16 g pro.

Herbed Egg-Potato Bake

You can assemble this cheesy dish up to two days ahead and refrigerate it.

PREP 30 minutes **BAKE** 1 hour 5 minutes **STAND** 10 minutes

    Butter
    ½ of a 32-ounce package frozen diced hash
        brown potatoes, thawed
    1 tablespoon butter
    1 small onion, chopped
    1 4-ounce can mushroom stems and pieces,
        drained
    6 eggs
    ¾ cup half-and-half or light cream
    3 tablespoons snipped fresh parsley
    1 tablespoon snipped fresh chives
    ½ teaspoon dried basil, crushed
    ½ teaspoon salt

    ½ teaspoon dry mustard
    ⅛ teaspoon ground black pepper
    ⅛ teaspoon cayenne pepper
    ½ cup shredded Monterey Jack cheese with
        jalapeño peppers, sharp cheddar cheese
        or Swiss cheese (2 ounces)

1. Generously butter an 8x8x2-inch (2-quart square) baking dish; set aside. Layer hash browns in prepared dish, building up sides; set aside.

2. In a medium skillet, melt the 1 tablespoon butter over medium heat. Add onion; cook until onion is tender, stirring occasionally. Spoon onion mixture and mushrooms over hash browns; set aside.

3. In a medium mixing bowl, beat eggs with a rotary beater or whisk. Beat or whisk in half-and-half, parsley, chives, basil, salt, dry mustard, black pepper and cayenne. Pour egg mixture evenly over onion mixture.

4. Bake, covered, in a 325° oven for 30 minutes. Uncover; bake about 35 minutes more, or until a knife inserted near the center comes out clean. Sprinkle with cheese. Let stand for 10 minutes before serving. **Makes 6 servings.**

Note: This recipe is easily doubled to serve 12. Double all the ingredients. Using a 13x9x2-inch baking dish, assemble recipe as directed. Bake, covered, for 30 minutes. Uncover; bake 35 minutes more, or until a knife inserted near center comes out clean. Sprinkle with cheese. Let stand 10 minutes.

Per serving: 244 cal, 13 g fat, 238 mg chol, 472 mg sodium, 19 g carbo, 2 g fiber, 12 g pro.

Jumbo Coffee Cake Muffins

PREP 20 minutes **BAKE** 25 minutes **COOL** 15 minutes

Nonstick cooking spray
1½ cups all-purpose flour
2 teaspoons baking powder
¼ teaspoon baking soda
¼ teaspoon salt
¼ cup shortening
1 8-ounce carton dairy sour cream or plain yogurt
½ cup granulated sugar
½ cup milk
1 beaten egg
¼ cup packed brown sugar
¼ cup chopped nuts
2 tablespoons granulated sugar
1 teaspoon ground cinnamon

1. Lightly coat six jumbo (3½-inch) muffin cups with cooking spray or line with paper bake cups. Set aside.

2. In a mixing bowl, combine the flour, baking powder, baking soda and salt. Cut in the shortening until the mixture is crumbly.

3. In another bowl, stir together the sour cream, the ½ cup sugar, the milk and egg. Add to the dry ingredients and stir just until combined.

4. In a small bowl, stir together the brown sugar, nuts, the 2 tablespoons sugar and the cinnamon.

5. Spoon half the batter into prepared muffin cups. Sprinkle half of the nut mixture into cups. Top with remaining batter and the remaining nut mixture.

6. Bake in a 350° oven for about 25 minutes or until a toothpick inserted in center comes out clean. Cool 15 minutes in pan on wire rack. Remove from pan and serve warm. **Makes 6 jumbo-size muffins.**

Note: For standard-size muffins, use twelve regular (2½-inch) muffin cups; divide batter evenly as above. Bake in 400° oven for 15 to 18 minutes. Cool 5 minutes. Remove from pans and serve warm.

Per muffin: 436 cal, 21 g fat, 54 mg chol, 328 mg sodium, 56 g carbo, 1 g fiber, 7 g pro.

Sour Cream-Cranberry Muffins

PREP 30 minutes **BAKE** 20 minutes
COOL 10 minutes

Nonstick cooking spray
1½ cups all-purpose flour
2 teaspoons baking powder
¼ teaspoon baking soda
¼ teaspoon salt
¼ cup butter
1 8-ounce carton dairy sour cream or plain yogurt
½ cup granulated sugar
½ cup milk
1 egg, lightly beaten
¾ cup dried cranberries
¼ cup packed brown sugar
¼ cup chopped pecans
2 tablespoons granulated sugar
1 teaspoon pumpkin pie spice

1. Lightly coat 12 regular (2½-inch) muffin cups with cooking spray. Set aside.

2. In a large mixing bowl, stir together the flour, baking powder, baking soda and salt. Cut in butter until mixture is crumbly.

3. In a medium bowl, stir together the sour cream, ½ cup sugar, milk and egg. Add to the dry ingredients and stir just until combined. Fold in the dried cranberries.

4. In a small bowl, stir together the brown sugar, pecans, 2 tablespoons granulated sugar and pumpkin pie spice.

5. Spoon half of the batter into muffin cups; sprinkle with half of the nut mixture. Top with remaining batter and nut mixture.

6. Bake in a 350° oven for 20 to 25 minutes or until a toothpick inserted in center comes out clean. Cool 10 minutes in pan on wire rack. Remove from pan and serve warm. **Makes 12 muffins.**

Per muffin: 234 cal, 10 g fat, 37 mg chol, 165 mg sodium, 33 g carbo, 1 g fiber, 3 g pro.

JUMBO COFFEE
CAKE MUFFINS

English Muffins in a Loaf with Honey Butter

PREP 35 minutes **RISE** 45 minutes
BAKE 25 minutes

   Cornmeal
6 cups all-purpose flour
2 packages active dry yeast
¼ teaspoon baking soda
2 cups milk
½ cup water
1 tablespoon sugar
1 teaspoon salt
   Cornmeal
   Honey Butter (optional; recipe follows)

1. Lightly grease two 8x4x2-inch loaf pans. Lightly sprinkle with cornmeal to coat bottom and sides. Set aside.

2. In a large mixing bowl, combine 3 cups of the flour, the yeast and baking soda; set aside. In a medium saucepan, heat and stir milk, the water, sugar and salt just until warm (120° to 130°). Add milk mixture to dry mixture; mix well using a wooden spoon. Stir in the remaining flour.

3. Divide the dough in half. Place dough in prepared loaf pans. Sprinkle tops with cornmeal. Cover; let rise in a warm place 45 minutes, or until double in size. Bake in a 400° oven for 25 minutes or until bread is golden. Immediately remove bread from pans. Cool on wire rack.

4. To serve, slice bread and toast. Serve with Honey Butter, if you like. **Makes 32 servings.**

Honey Butter: In a small bowl, beat ½ cup softened butter and ¼ cup honey with an electric mixer on low speed until well mixed. Store in refrigerator.

Per serving: 90 cal, 1 g fat, 1 mg chol, 91 mg sodium, 18 g carbo, 1 g fiber, 3 g pro.

Cranberry Scones

Coarsely chopped cranberries spread sweet-tart flavor throughout this tender scone. Almond frosting complements the berries.

PREP 25 minutes **BAKE** 12 minutes

   1 cup fresh or frozen cranberries
2½ cups all-purpose flour
⅔ cup sugar
2½ teaspoons baking powder
½ teaspoon baking soda
¾ cup cold butter, sliced
¾ cup buttermilk
   Almond Frosting (recipe follows)

1. Rinse cranberries in cold water; drain. Slice or coarsely chop cranberries; set aside. Lightly grease two baking sheets or line with parchment paper; set aside.

2. In a large bowl, combine flour, sugar, baking powder and baking soda. Using a pastry blender, cut in the butter pieces until mixture resembles coarse crumbs. Make a well in center of the flour mixture; set aside.

3. In a medium bowl, combine buttermilk and cranberries. Add buttermilk mixture all at once to flour mixture. Stir just until combined.

4. Turn dough out onto a lightly floured surface. Knead dough by folding and gently pressing it for 10 to 12 strokes or until dough is nearly smooth. Divide dough in half. Pat or lightly roll each dough half into an 8-inch circle that's about ½ inch thick. Cut each circle into eight wedges.

5. Place dough wedges 2 inches apart on prepared baking sheets. Bake in a 400° oven for 12 to 14 minutes or until scones are golden brown on top. Scones may spread slightly when baked. Transfer scones to wire racks to cool slightly. Spread tops with Almond Frosting and serve warm. **Makes 16 scones.**

Almond Frosting: In a medium mixing bowl, beat 1 tablespoon butter, softened, and ½ teaspoon almond extract with an electric mixer on medium speed for 30 seconds. Gradually add 1½ cups powdered sugar and 2 tablespoons milk, beating until well combined and scraping the sides of the bowl often.

Per scone: 239 cal, 10 g fat, 25 mg chol, 157 mg sodium, 36 g carbo, 1 g fiber, 3 g pro.

CRANBERRY
SCONES

Chocolate-Nut Cinnamon Rolls

Who can resist a good sticky roll—especially when it's this easy to make? Starting with frozen bread dough, we added brown sugar, cinnamon, nuts and chocolate. Need we say more?

PREP 30 minutes **RISE** 30 minutes **BAKE** 30 minutes **COOL** 5 minutes

  2 cups powdered sugar
 ⅔ cup whipping cream
1½ cups chopped mixed nuts
 ½ cup packed brown sugar
  1 tablespoon all-purpose flour
  1 tablespoon ground cinnamon
  2 16-ounce loaves frozen sweet rolls or
       white bread dough, thawed
 ¼ cup butter, melted
1¼ cups semisweet chocolate pieces
1½ teaspoons shortening

1. For topping: In a medium bowl, stir together powdered sugar and whipping cream until smooth. Divide mixture between two 2-quart rectangular or square baking dishes. Sprinkle 1 cup of the chopped nuts evenly over mixture in baking dishes; set aside.

2. For filling: In a small bowl, stir together brown sugar, flour and cinnamon; set aside.

3. On a lightly floured surface, roll each loaf of dough into a 12x8-inch rectangle (if dough is difficult to roll out, let it rest a few minutes and try again). Brush dough rectangles with melted butter. Sprinkle filling, ½ cup of the chocolate pieces, and the remaining ½ cup chopped nuts over each rectangle. Roll up each rectangle, starting from a long side. Pinch dough to seal seams. Slice each roll into six equal pieces. Arrange six pieces, cut sides down, in each prepared dish. Cover and let rise in a warm place until nearly double in size (30 to 45 minutes). Use a greased toothpick to break any surface bubbles.

4. Bake in a 375° oven for 30 to 35 minutes or until sides of rolls are brown and center rolls do not appear doughy (do not underbake). If necessary to prevent overbrowning, cover with foil during the last 15 or 20 minutes of baking. Cool in dishes on wire racks for 5 minutes; remove from dishes.

5. In a small saucepan, combine the remaining ¾ cup chocolate pieces and the shortening. Cook and stir over low heat until chocolate is melted and smooth; drizzle over cinnamon rolls. Serve warm. **Makes 12 rolls.**

Per roll: 586 cal, 27 g fat, 72 mg chol, 176 mg sodium, 80 g carbo, 4 g fiber, 10 g pro.

Savor the crunch of the snow, the sound of the saw, the scent of pine, and the camaraderie of finding a tree together.

Hot Artichoke and Roasted Pepper Asiago Cheese Dip

PREP 25 minutes **BAKE** 25 minutes

1 8-ounce package cream cheese, softened
4 ounces Asiago or Parmesan cheese, finely shredded (1 cup)
2 cloves garlic
1 13- to 14-ounce can artichoke hearts, drained
1 cup bottled roasted red sweet peppers, drained
1 cup sliced fresh mushrooms
½ cup sliced green onions
    Thinly sliced French bread, toasted, or toasted pita wedges
    Chopped roasted red sweet peppers (optional)
    Parsley leaves (optional)

1. In a food processor bowl, combine cream cheese, Asiago cheese and garlic. Cover and process until mixture is well combined. Add drained artichoke hearts, drained sweet red peppers, mushrooms and green onions. Cover and process with on/off turns until finely chopped.

2. Transfer dip to an 8-inch quiche dish or 9-inch pie plate, spreading evenly. Bake, covered, in a 350° oven for 25 minutes or until heated through. Or microwave, uncovered, on 70 percent power (medium-high) for 6 to 8 minutes or until heated through, stirring the dip and turning the dish halfway through cooking time. Serve warm with thinly sliced French bread. Garnish with additional red pepper and parsley, if you like. **Makes 12 servings.**

Per serving: 126 cal, 10 g fat, 31 mg chol, 271 mg sodium, 4 g carbo, 2 g fiber, 5 g pro.

Cranberry-Sauced Meatballs

PREP 30 minutes **BAKE** 15 minutes **COOK** 2 to 3 hours on low or 1 to 1½ hours on high

    Nonstick cooking spray
1 egg
½ cup seasoned fine dry bread crumbs
½ cup dried cranberries, snipped, or golden raisins, snipped
¼ cup finely chopped onion
1 teaspoon salt
½ teaspoon garlic powder
½ teaspoon ground cloves or allspice
2 pounds uncooked ground chicken or turkey
1 16-ounce can jellied cranberry sauce
1 cup bottled barbecue sauce

1. Lightly coat a 15x10x1-inch baking pan with nonstick cooking spray; set aside. For meatballs: In a very large bowl, beat egg with a fork. Stir in bread crumbs, dried cranberries, onion, salt, garlic powder and cloves. Add ground chicken; mix well. Shape into 60 meatballs.

2. Place meatballs in prepared pan. Bake in a 350° oven for 15 to 18 minutes or until done (165°).

3. Meanwhile, in a 3½- to 4-quart slow cooker, stir together cranberry sauce and barbecue sauce. Add cooked meatballs, stirring gently to coat. Cover and cook on low-heat setting for 2 to 3 hours or on high-heat setting for 1 to 1½ hours. (Meatballs may be kept warm on low-heat setting for up to 1 hour more.) Serve with toothpicks. **Makes 60 meatballs.**

Per meatball: 48 cal, 1 g fat, 17 mg chol, 122 mg sodium, 6 g carbo, 0 g fiber, 3 g pro.

Swiss-Artichoke Dip

This sports bar favorite has been deliciously adapted to the slow cooker. Process Swiss cheese is the ticket here—traditional cheese can break down when slow-cooked.

PREP 15 minutes **COOK** 2½ hours to 3 hours on low or 1½ hours on high

1 8- to 9-ounce package frozen artichoke hearts, thawed and chopped
2 3-ounce packages cream cheese, cut up
2 ounces process Swiss cheese slices, torn into small pieces
¼ cup snipped dried tomatoes (not oil packed)
¼ cup mayonnaise
¼ cup milk
1 teaspoon dried minced onion
1 clove garlic, minced
    Crackers or baguette slices, toasted

1. In a 1½-quart slow cooker, combine artichoke hearts, cream cheese, Swiss cheese, dried tomatoes, mayonnaise, milk, dried onion and garlic.

2. Cover and cook on low-heat setting for 2½ to 3 hours or on high-heat setting for 1½ hours. If no heat setting is available, cook for 1½ hours.

3. Stir before serving. Serve dip with crackers. **Makes 12 (¼ cup) servings.**

Per serving: 113 cal, 10 g fat, 22 mg chol, 173 mg sodium, 3 g carbo, 1 g fiber, 3 g pro.

SWISS-ARTICHOKE DIP
AND CRANBERRY-
SAUCED MEATBALLS

FESTIVE
CRANBERRY
BRIE

Festive Cranberry Brie

PREP 25 minutes **COOK** 15 minutes
BAKE 10 minutes

- 2 cups fresh or frozen cranberries
- ¾ cup water
- ½ cup granulated sugar
- ¼ cup packed brown sugar
- ½ teaspoon ground cinnamon
- ½ teaspoon ground ginger
- Dash ground cloves
- Dash ground allspice
- 1 medium Granny Smith apple, peeled, cored and chopped
- ¼ cup golden raisins
- 2 8-ounce rounds Brie cheese
- Assorted crackers or sliced and toasted baguette
- Pear slices (optional)

1. Preheat oven to 350°. Rinse cranberries in cold water; drain.

2. For the cranberry chutney: In a small saucepan, stir together the water, granulated sugar and brown sugar. Bring to boiling, stirring to dissolve sugar. Boil rapidly for 5 minutes. Stir in cranberries, cinnamon, ginger, cloves and allspice. Return to boiling; reduce heat. Simmer, uncovered, for 5 minutes, stirring occasionally. Stir in apple and raisins. Simmer, uncovered, about 5 minutes more or until desired consistency. If desired, cool to room temperature.

3. Meanwhile, place Brie in an oven-safe serving dish. Bake, uncovered, for 10 to 15 minutes or until cheese is warm and slightly softened.

4. To serve, spoon the cranberry chutney over the warmed Brie. Serve with crackers and if you like, pears. **Makes 8 servings.**

Per serving: 372 cal, 19 g fat, 57 mg chol, 511 mg sodium, 38 g carbo, 2 g fiber, 13 g pro.

Pear-Shape Sake Cheese Ball

PREP 50 minutes **CHILL** 6 to 24 hours **STAND** 15 minutes

- 2 8-ounce packages cream cheese
- 1 8-ounce package Camembert cheese, rind removed and cut up
- 1 cup shredded aged white cheddar, provolone or Swiss cheese (4 ounces)
- ¼ cup butter
- ¼ cup sake, dry white wine or milk
- 2 tablespoons apricot or peach preserves
- ¼ teaspoon ground white pepper or black pepper
- ½ cup slivered almonds, toasted and chopped
- ⅓ cup grated Parmesan cheese or Romano cheese
- 1 inch stick cinnamon
- 1 small fresh bay leaf
- Sesame crackers, celery stalks, cucumber slices, Bosc or Anjou pear slices, apple wedges and/or dried apricot halves

1. In a large mixing bowl, let cream cheese, Camembert, shredded cheddar and butter come to room temperature for 45 minutes. Add sake, apricot preserves and pepper. Beat with an electric mixer on medium speed until almost smooth. Stir in almonds.

2. Cover and chill cheese mixture about 2 hours or until easy to handle. Shape mixture into a round ball. Shake Parmesan cheese onto a piece of waxed paper; roll ball in cheese. For a pear, mold the round cheese ball into a pear shape (if making pear shape, sprinkle with the Parmesan cheese after shaping). Cover with plastic wrap. Chill for 4 to 24 hours.

3. To serve, place pear-shape or the round cheese ball in a large shallow serving bowl or on a platter. For the pear, make a small depression in the top for stem end. Insert cinnamon stick in pear for stem and the bay leaf. Let stand for 15 minutes before serving. Arrange crackers, celery, cucumber, pear or apples and/or apricots around the cheese. **Makes 16 (¼-cup) servings.**

Per serving: 229 cal, 20 g fat, 58 mg chol, 301 mg sodium, 4 g carbo, 0 g fiber, 8 g pro.

STUFFED PARTY
PINWHEELS

Stuffed Party Pinwheels

PREP 30 minutes **CHILL** 4 to 24 hours

½ cup mayonnaise
½ teaspoon curry powder
1 5.2-ounce container semisoft cream
    cheese with garlic and herb
2 teaspoons milk
6 8- to 9-inch jalapeño and cilantro, dried
    tomato and basil, and/or spinach and
    vegetable flour tortillas
½ to ¾ pound very thinly sliced cooked
    chicken, roast beef and/or salami
⅔ cup bottled roasted red sweet peppers,
    drained and cut into very thin strips
⅔ cup lightly packed fresh basil leaves

1. In a small bowl, combine mayonnaise
and curry powder; set aside. In another
small bowl, combine semisoft cheese and
milk; set aside.

2. Spread three tortillas with the curry
mixture. Spread remaining three tortillas
with the cheese mixture. Arrange chicken,
roast beef and/or salami over each tortilla.
Top with pepper strips and fresh basil,
arranging basil leaves 1 to 2 inches apart.
Roll up each tortilla tightly into a spiral.
Wrap in plastic wrap. Chill for 4 to 24 hours.

3. To serve, remove the plastic wrap from
the rolls. Trim ends from the tortillas. Slice
rolls diagonally into 1½- to 2-inch slices.
Makes 24 servings.

Per serving: 105 cal, 7 g fat, 10 mg chol, 107 mg
sodium, 6 g carbo, 0 g fiber, 4 g pro.

Hot Buttered Rum

START TO FINISH 15 minutes

1 pint vanilla ice cream, softened
2 sticks butter, softened
1 cup powdered sugar
1 cup packed brown sugar
¾ teaspoon ground cinnamon
¾ teaspoon ground nutmeg

1. For base: In a medium mixing bowl,
combine all ingredients. Beat with a mixer
until smooth (you may have a few very
small pieces of butter left). Transfer to a
freezer container and freeze until ready to
use. Hot Buttered Rum base may be used
right away or frozen for up to 3 months.

2. To serve, place 1 to 2 tablespoons of the
base and 1 to 2 tablespoons of amber or
clear rum in a coffee mug and top with
boiling water. Stir until base is dissolved.
Sprinkle with additional nutmeg, if you
like, and add a cinnamon stick. **Makes
35 servings.**

Per serving: 107 cal, 7 g fat, 23 mg chol, 47 mg
sodium, 11 g carbo, 0 g fiber, 0 g pro.

Note: For Hot Buttered Coffee, omit the
rum in base and add hot brewed coffee
instead of the water.

Spiced Pear Tea

START TO FINISH 25 minutes

1 orange
3 cups pear nectar
3 cups water
4 inches stick cinnamon
1 teaspoon whole cloves
6 regular-size tea bags
¼ cup honey
    Small orange slices (optional)
    Cinnamon sticks (optional)

1. Use a vegetable peeler to remove three
wide strips of peel from the orange; set peel
aside. Squeeze juice from orange.

2. In a large saucepan, combine pear nectar,
the water and orange juice. For the spice
bag, place cinnamon, cloves and the orange
peel strips in the center of a 6-inch square
of double-thick 100-percent-cotton
cheesecloth. Bring corners together and tie
with a clean string. Add bag to pear nectar
mixture.

3. Bring mixture to boiling; reduce heat.
Cover and simmer 10 minutes. Remove
from heat. Add tea bags; cover and let stand
5 minutes. Remove tea bags and spice bag
and discard. Stir in honey. Serve in mugs.
If you like, float orange slices on top of each
serving and serve with cinnamon stick
stirrers. **Makes 8 (6 ounce) servings.**

Per serving: 93 cal, 0 g fat, 0 mg chol, 6 mg sodium,
24 g carbo, 1 g fiber, 0 g pro.

Punch with a Punch

This punch gets its kick from tequila. If you'd like a nonalcoholic option, use lemon-lime carbonated beverage instead of the tequila.

PREP 10 minutes

- 1 46-ounce can punch drink, chilled
- 1 6-ounce can frozen orange juice concentrate, thawed
- 1 6-ounce can frozen lemonade concentrate, thawed
- 1 750-milliliter bottle tequila or rum, chilled
  Sliced fresh limes (optional)

1. In a very large pitcher or bowl, combine punch, orange juice, lemonade and tequila; mix well.

2. To serve, pour punch over crushed ice. Garnish with lime slices, if you like. **Makes 10 (8 ounce) servings.**

Per serving: 288 cal, 0 g fat, 0 mg chol, 33 mg sodium, 31 g carbo, 0 g fiber, 0 g pro.

Seduction Martini

PREP 5 minutes

- Ice cubes
- 3 ounces pineapple juice (6 tablespoons)
- 3 ounces cranberry juice (6 tablespoons)
- 2½ ounces Three Olives Berry Vodka (⅓ cup)
- ½ ounce Simple Syrup (1 tablespoon)
- ½ ounce Pama Pomegranate Liqueur (1 tablespoon)
- Star fruit (carambola), slices

Place ice cubes in a cocktail shaker; add all ingredients except star fruit. Cover and shake vigorously for 10 to 15 seconds or until a light frost develops on the outside of the cocktail shaker. Strain into two martini glasses. Garnish each with a slice of star fruit. **Makes 2 (5 ounce) servings.**

Per serving: 167 cal, 0 g fat, 0 mg chol, 2 mg sodium, 19 g carbo, 0 g fiber, 0 g pro.

Simple Syrup: In a small saucepan, combine ½ cup sugar and ½ cup water. Cook and stir over medium heat until sugar dissolves. Transfer to a small bowl or a 1 cup glass measure. Cover and chill for 1 hour before using. Makes ¾ cup.

Old Blue Eyes Martini

This cocktail gets its blue hue from Blue Curacao, an orange-flavor liqueur to which color is added.

START TO FINISH 10 minutes

- 1 cup ice cubes
- 5 ounces cranberry juice (⅔ cup)
- 2 ounces Pearl Blueberry Vodka (¼ cup)
- 1 ounce Blue Curacao (2 tablespoons)
- ½ ounce Simple Syrup (1 tablespoon) (see recipe, below left)
- ½ ounce lime juice (1 tablespoon)
- Blueberries

Place ice cubes in a cocktail shaker; add all ingredients except blueberries. Cover; shake vigorously for at least 10 to 15 seconds or until a light frost develops on the outside of the cocktail shaker. Strain into two martini glasses. Garnish each with blueberries. **Makes 2 (5 ounce) servings.**

Per serving: 164 cal, 0 g fat, 0 mg chol, 2 mg sodium, 20 g carbo, 0 g fiber, 0 g pro.

Having something to sip—hot or cold—keeps party guests happy and nibbling. Be sure to stock plenty of interesting nonalcoholic options.

SEDUCTION
MARTINI AND OLD
BLUE EYES MARTINI

Wine-Marinated Pot Roast

Proving a familiar favorite can always find its elegant side, this tender braised beef dish features a gorgeous, glossy red wine sauce that amps up sweet root vegetables, mushrooms and onion.

PREP 45 minutes **MARINATE** 8 to 24 hours **BAKE** 3 hours 30 minutes

1 3- to 3½-pound boneless beef chuck arm pot roast, beef chuck shoulder pot roast or beef chuck seven-bone pot roast

1 750-milliliter bottle fruity red wine (such as Cabernet Sauvignon, red Zinfandel or Merlot)

½ teaspoon kosher salt, sea salt or salt

½ teaspoon ground black pepper

2 tablespoons olive oil or vegetable oil

1 10.5-ounce can condensed beef broth

¼ cup no-salt-added tomato paste

1 tablespoon Dijon-style mustard

1 tablespoon herbes de Provence, fines herbes or Italian seasoning, crushed

3 cloves garlic, chopped

2 bay leaves

1 large onion, cut into thin wedges

4 medium carrots, peeled, cut in half lengthwise and halved crosswise, or 2 cups packaged peeled fresh baby carrots

4 medium parsnips, peeled and cut into 2-inch pieces, or 4 medium potatoes, peeled and cut lengthwise into sixths

2 cups whole fresh cremini mushrooms

2 stalks celery, bias-sliced into 1-inch pieces

Hot cooked noodles

2 tablespoons snipped Italian (flat-leaf) parsley

Baguette-style French bread, cut into 1½-inch slices (optional)

1. Trim fat from meat. Place meat in a resealable plastic bag set in a shallow dish. Pour wine over meat; seal bag. Marinate in the refrigerator for at least 8 hours and up to 24 hours, turning bag occasionally.

2. Drain meat, reserving wine. Pat meat dry with paper towels. Sprinkle meat with salt and black pepper. In a 4- to 6-quart Dutch oven, over medium heat, brown meat on all sides in hot oil.

3. In a medium saucepan, bring reserved wine to boiling; reduce heat. Simmer, uncovered, for 15 to 20 minutes or until wine is reduced by half, to about 1½ cups. Stir in beef broth, tomato paste, mustard, herbes de Provence, garlic and bay leaves. Return to boiling; reduce heat. Simmer, uncovered for 5 minutes more. Pour wine mixture over meat in Dutch oven; add onion.

4. Bake, covered, in a 325° oven for 2½ hours. Add carrots, parsnips, mushrooms and celery. Bake, covered, about 1 hour more or until meat is very tender. Transfer meat and vegetables to a large serving platter, reserving juices in Dutch oven. Cover meat and vegetables with foil to keep warm.

5. For wine sauce, skim off any fat from juices. Bring to boiling; reduce heat. Simmer, uncovered, for 10 to 15 minutes or until juices are slightly thickened. Season to taste.

6. Slice meat or use a fork to break meat apart into pieces. Serve wine sauce with meat, vegetables and noodles. Sprinkle meat and vegetables with parsley. If you like, serve with French bread. **Makes 8 servings.**

Per serving: 578 cal, 26 g fat, 108 mg chol, 760 mg sodium, 37 g carbo, 5 g fiber, 33 g pro.

Beef Short Ribs over Gorgonzola Polenta

What is your slow cooker but a braising machine? Short ribs aren't that expensive, but cooked this way, they give you a delicious, dressed-up dish with hardly any work. A hint of licorice from fennel accents the dish.

PREP 50 minutes **COOK** 9 to 10 hours on low or 4½ to 5 hours on high

2½ to 3 pounds boneless beef short ribs
2 large onions, cut into thin wedges
1 cup thinly sliced carrots (2 medium)
1 medium fennel bulb, cored and cut into
   thin wedges
1 14.5-ounce can diced tomatoes, undrained
1 cup dry red wine
2 tablespoons quick-cooking tapioca,
   crushed
2 tablespoons tomato paste
1 teaspoon dried rosemary, crushed
1 teaspoon salt
½ teaspoon ground black pepper
4 cloves garlic, minced
   Cheesy Polenta (recipe follows)

1. Trim fat from meat. In a 5- or 6-quart slow cooker, combine onions, carrots and fennel. Top with meat.

2. In a small bowl, combine undrained tomatoes, wine, tapioca, tomato paste, dried rosemary, salt, pepper and garlic. Pour over meat and vegetables.

3. Cover and cook on low-heat setting for 9 to 10 hours or on high-heat setting for 4½ to 5 hours.

4. Meanwhile, prepare Cheesy Polenta. Spoon polenta into shallow bowls. Spoon meat and vegetables over polenta.
Makes 6 servings.

Cheesy Polenta: In a large saucepan, bring 2½ cups water to boiling. Meanwhile, in a bowl, stir together 1 cup coarse-ground yellow cornmeal, 1 cup cold water and ½ teaspoon salt. Slowly add cornmeal mixture to boiling water, stirring constantly. Cook and stir until mixture returns to boiling. Reduce heat to medium-low. Cook for 25 to 30 minutes or until very thick, stirring frequently and adjusting heat as necessary to maintain a very slow boil. Stir in ⅓ cup crumbled Gorgonzola cheese, blue cheese or shredded Parmesan cheese.

Per serving: 502 cal, 18 g fat, 113 mg chol, 993 mg sodium, 35 g carbo, 6 g fiber, 42 g pro.

Slow-cooked meat dishes infused with herbs, vegetables, and wine—whether braised in the oven or in the slow cooker—fill the house with warm, welcoming aromas.

Fireside Beef Stew with Root Vegetables

PREP 1 hour   **COOK** 10 to 12 hours on low or 5 to 6 hours on high

1 2- to 2½-pound boneless beef chuck
  pot roast
1 tablespoon olive oil or vegetable oil
½ of a 2-ounce package onion soup mix
  (1 envelope)
2 medium sweet potatoes, peeled and cut
  into 1-inch pieces (2½ cups)
2 cups packaged peeled baby carrots,
  halved lengthwise, or 4 medium carrots,
  halved lengthwise and cut into 1-inch
  pieces (2 cups)
2 medium potatoes, peeled and chopped
  (about 2 cups)
2 medium parsnips, peeled, halved
  lengthwise and cut into 1-inch pieces
  (1¼ cups)

1 medium turnip, peeled, quartered and
  sliced ¾ inch thick (1¼ cups)
4 cloves garlic, minced
2 14.5-ounce cans reduced-sodium beef
  broth
1 cup cranberry juice or cranberry-apple
  drink
3 tablespoons quick-cooking tapioca
1 teaspoon ground turmeric
1 teaspoon ground cumin
¼ to ½ teaspoon cayenne pepper
  Thinly sliced green onions or snipped
  fresh chives (optional)
  Sour cream (optional)

1. Trim fat from meat. Cut meat into 1-inch pieces. In a large skillet, cook meat, half at a time, in hot oil over medium heat until browned on all sides, turning to brown evenly. Transfer meat to a 5- to 6-quart slow cooker; add soup mix and toss to coat. Add sweet potatoes, carrots, potatoes, parsnips, turnip and garlic.

2. In a medium bowl, combine beef broth, cranberry juice, tapioca, turmeric, cumin and cayenne pepper. Pour over meat mixture in cooker.

3. Cover and cook on low-heat setting for 10 to 12 hours or on high-heat setting for 5 to 6 hours.

4. If you like, garnish each serving with green onions and serve with sour cream. **Makes 8 servings.**

Per serving: 396 cal, 19 g fat, 71 mg chol, 622 mg sodium, 30 g carbo, 4 g fiber, 25 g pro.

Make-ahead tip: Meat can be cut into 1-inch pieces and refrigerated overnight. Sweet potatoes, carrots, potatoes, parsnips and turnips can be cut up the night before. Place in a very large bowl of water; cover and chill.

Zippy Holiday Pork Roast

Habanero chili pepper sparks this Caribbean-style marinade. It's delicious on chicken as well as pork.

PREP 30 minutes **MARINATE** 2 hours
ROAST 1 hour 45 minutes **STAND** 15 minutes

- 2 tablespoons dried thyme, crushed
- 1 tablespoon ground allspice
- 1 tablespoon black pepper
- 4 teaspoons onion powder
- 2 teaspoons crushed and dried habanero chili pepper, crushed red pepper or crushed dried jalapeño pepper
- 1 teaspoon kosher salt
- 2 cups chicken stock or broth
- 1 3-pound boneless pork top loin roast (single loin)

1. In a medium saucepan, combine thyme, allspice, black pepper, onion powder, chili pepper and salt. Stir in stock. Bring to boiling. Cool.

2. Place pork roast in a plastic bag set in a shallow dish. Pour cooled marinade over meat and close bag. Marinate in refrigerator for at least 2 hours before roasting or grilling.

3. Drain pork, discarding marinade. Place roast on a rack in a shallow roasting pan. Insert an oven-safe meat thermometer. Roast in a 325° oven for about 1¾ hours or until thermometer registers 155°. (Or in a grill with a cover, arrange preheated coals around a drip pan. Place meat on a rack in a roasting pan on the grill rack over medium-low heat. Cover and grill 1 to 1¼ hours or until thermometer registers 155°.)

4. Cover the meat with foil. Let it stand for 15 minutes before carving (the meat's temperature will rise 5° while it stands). **Makes 8 servings.**

Per serving: 208 cal, 11 g fat, 77 mg chol, 175 mg sodium, 1 g carbo, 0 g fiber,

Note: This recipe may be made with chicken. Substitute 2 to 2½ pounds meaty chicken pieces (breasts, thighs and drumsticks) for pork roast. Marinate as directed. To cook, place chicken pieces, bone sides up, on the unheated rack of a broiler pan. Broil 4 to 5 inches from the heat for about 20 minutes or until lightly browned. Turn chicken. Broil for 5 to 15 minutes more or until the chicken is no longer pink. Or in a grill with a cover, arrange preheated coals around a drip pan. Test for medium heat above the pan. Place chicken, bone sides down, on grill rack over drip pan. Cover and grill for 50 to 60 minutes or until chicken is tender and no longer pink.

Roast Breast of Chicken with Mushroom and Wild Rice Stuffing

To make soft bread crumbs, tear up a piece of soft white bread—crusts are fine to include—and pulse it a few times in a food processor.

PREP 40 minutes **BAKE** 30 minutes
CHILL 2 hours

- 2 tablespoons butter
- ¼ cup finely chopped onion
- ¼ cup finely chopped celery
- 1 small clove garlic, minced
- 8 ounces fresh mushrooms, finely chopped
- ¼ cup whipping cream or heavy cream
- 1 cup cooked wild rice
- ⅓ cup soft bread crumbs (½ slice)
- ¼ teaspoon salt
- ⅛ teaspoon freshly ground black pepper
- 6 skinless, boneless chicken breast halves (1½ pounds total)
  Nonstick cooking spray

1. For stuffing: In large skillet, cook onion, celery and garlic in 1 tablespoon of the butter over medium heat for 8 to 10 minutes or until tender, stirring occasionally. Add mushrooms. Cook over medium-high heat for 6 to 8 minutes or until mushrooms are tender and most of the liquid is evaporated, stirring occasionally. Add cream. Bring to boiling; reduce heat. Simmer, uncovered, for 3 minutes. Stir in rice, bread crumbs, ¼ teaspoon salt and ⅛ teaspoon pepper. Cover and chill at least 2 hours before using.

2. Make a horizontal pocket in each chicken breast half by cutting from one side almost to, but not through, the other side. Spoon chilled stuffing into chicken pockets. Don't worry if the stuffing isn't totally enclosed by the chicken.

3. Line a 15x10x1-inch baking pan with foil; coat foil with nonstick cooking spray. Arrange stuffed chicken breast halves in foil-lined pan.

4. Melt the remaining 1 tablespoon butter and brush on chicken breast halves. Season with additional salt and black pepper. Bake, uncovered, in a 375° oven for 30 to 35 minutes or until internal temperature of chicken breast halves reaches 170° on an instant-read thermometer. **Makes 6 servings.**

Make-ahead tip: Prepare as above through Step 3. Cover and chill stuffed chicken breast halves up to 24 hours. Uncover and continue as directed in Step 4.

Per serving: 240 cal, 9 g fat, 90 mg chol, 225 mg sodium, 10 g carbo, 1 g fiber, 29 g pro.

Warming foods such as stews and soup can be cooked over a fire during an outdoor winter party. It's a wonderful way to enjoy the weather.

Wild Rice and Chicken Soup

Prep for this Midwestern favorite is simplified with a can of soup, a package of long grain and wild rice mix and a slow cooker. (Pictured on page 208.)

PREP 20 minutes **COOK** 6 to 8 hours on low or 3 to 4 hours on high

2½ cups chopped cooked chicken
2 cups sliced fresh mushrooms
2 medium carrots, coarsely shredded
2 stalks celery, sliced
1 10¾-ounce can reduced-fat and reduced-sodium condensed cream of chicken soup or cream of mushroom soup
1 6-ounce package long grain and wild rice mix
5 cups reduced-sodium chicken broth
5 cups water
   Celery leaves (optional)

1. In a 5- to 6-quart slow cooker, combine cooked chicken, mushrooms, carrots, celery, cream of chicken soup, rice and the contents of the rice seasoning packet. Gradually stir in chicken broth and the water.

2. Cover slow cooker; cook on low-heat setting for 6 to 8 hours or on high-heat setting for 3 to 4 hours. Garnish with celery leaves, if you like. **Makes 8 to 10 servings.**

Per serving: 203 cal, 5 g fat, 42 mg chol, 875 mg sodium, 23 g carbo, 2 g fiber, 18 g pro.

Southwestern Potato-Sausage Chowder

Feed a houseful with this simple slow-cooker soup. Vary the spiciness by choosing sweet or hot sausage and serrano or jalapeño pepper. (Pictured on page 208.)

PREP 30 minutes **COOK** 8 to 10 hours on low or 4 to 5 hours on high

1 pound bulk pork sausage
1 pound round red potatoes, chopped
1 large onion, chopped
1 medium red sweet pepper, chopped
1 green sweet pepper, chopped
1 serrano or jalapeño pepper, seeded and chopped (optional; see Note, page 58)
2 cloves garlic, minced
2 teaspoons ground cumin
¼ teaspoon ground black pepper
2 14-ounce cans reduced-sodium chicken broth
   Shredded Monterey Jack cheese with jalapeño peppers (optional)
1 cup canned shoestring potatoes (optional)

1. In a large skillet, cook sausage until no longer pink; drain off fat.

2. In a 3½- or 4-quart slow cooker, combine cooked sausage, potatoes, onion, sweet peppers, serrano pepper (if using), garlic, cumin and ground pepper. Stir in chicken broth.

3. Cover and cook on low-heat setting for 8 to 10 hours or on high-heat setting for 4 to 5 hours. Top each serving with cheese and/or shoestring potatoes, if you like. **Makes 6 servings.**

Per serving: 322 cal, 20 g fat, 54 mg chol, 804 mg sodium, 19 g carbo, 3 g fiber, 15 g pro.

Cheesy Potato Soup

There's nothing fancy or surprising about this simple soup. It's tried and true; kids of all ages call it a favorite. (Pictured on page 209.)

PREP 25 minutes **COOK** 9 to 10 hours on low or 4½ to 5 hours on high

6 medium potatoes, peeled and chopped (6 cups)
2½ cups water
½ cup chopped onion
2 teaspoons instant chicken bouillon granules
¼ teaspoon ground black pepper
1½ cups shredded American cheese (6 ounces)
1 12-ounce can (1½ cups) evaporated milk
   Cooked, crumbled bacon (optional)
   Sliced green onions (optional)

1. In a 3½- or 4-quart slow cooker, combine potatoes, the water, onion, bouillon granules and pepper. Cover; cook on low-heat setting for 8 to 9 hours or on high-heat setting 4 to 4½ hours.

2. Stir cheese and milk into mixture in cooker. Cover; cook on low-heat setting for 1 hour more or on high-heat setting for 30 minutes more. For a thicker soup, mash potatoes slightly. If you like, sprinkle each serving with bacon and green onions. **Makes 4 servings.**

For 5- or 6-quart slow cooker: Use 8 medium potatoes, peeled and chopped; 4 cups water; ¾ cup chopped onion; 1 tablespoon instant chicken bouillon granules; ¼ teaspoon pepper; 2 cups shredded American cheese (8 ounces); and one 12-ounce can evaporated milk plus one 5-ounce can evaporated milk. Prepare as above. **Makes 6 main-dish or 8 to 10 side-dish servings.**

Per serving: 500 cal, 20 g fat, 65 mg chol, 1,132 mg sodium, 62 g carbo, 5 g fiber, 20 g pro.

SOUTHWESTERN
POTATO-SAUSAGE
CHOWDER

WILD RICE AND
CHICKEN SOUP

CHEESY
POTATO SOUP

Warm-Me-Up Chicken Chili

Serve this tasty chili with warm corn bread or corn muffins and a green salad.

PREP 35 minutes **COOK** 40 minutes

2 tablespoons olive oil or vegetable oil

2 pounds skinless, boneless chicken breast halves or thighs, cut into 1-inch pieces*

1 large onion, chopped (1 cup)

2 celery stalks, chopped (1 cup)

1 large green or red sweet pepper, seeded and chopped (1 cup)

2 medium yellow banana peppers or poblano chile peppers, seeded and chopped (1 cup) (see Note, page 58)

3 medium cloves garlic, minced

2 tablespoons ground cumin

1 tablespoon chili powder

1 tablespoon dried oregano, crushed

½ to ¾ teaspoon crushed red pepper

¼ teaspoon salt

1 28-ounce can or two 15-ounce cans tomato puree

2 14.5-ounce cans diced tomatoes

1 15- to 16-ounce can black beans, rinsed and drained

1 15- to 16-ounce pinto beans or dark red kidney beans, rinsed and drained

Assorted toppings (such as snipped fresh cilantro or parsley, sour cream, corn chips, lime wedges, shredded cheddar and/or Monterey Jack cheese, finely chopped red onion, sliced green onions and/or bottled green salsa)

1. In a 5- or 6-quart Dutch oven, heat the oil over medium-high heat. Add half of the chicken pieces; cook and stir for 4 to 5 minutes or until no longer pink. Remove with a slotted spoon. Repeat with remaining chicken, removing all chicken from pan when cooked.

2. In the Dutch oven, add onion, celery, sweet pepper, banana peppers and garlic. Cook for 5 to 6 minutes or until the onion is tender, stirring occasionally. Stir in cumin, chili powder, oregano, crushed red pepper and salt. Cook and stir for 2 minutes more. Return chicken to the Dutch oven.

3. Add tomato puree and undrained tomatoes to Dutch oven; stir to combine. Bring to boiling; reduce heat. Simmer, covered, for 30 minutes, stirring occasionally. Stir in the drained black and pinto beans. Simmer, covered, for 10 minutes more. Season to taste.

4. To serve, ladle into soup bowls and sprinkle with assorted toppings. **Makes 6 servings.**

Per serving: 449 cal, 8 g fat, 88 mg chol, 1,504 mg sodium, 51 g carbo, 16 g fiber, 51 g pro.

*Note: To save time, omit Step 1 and substitute 3½ cups cubed cooked chicken or turkey for the 2 pounds skinless, boneless chicken breast halves or thighs.

Chili has nearly as many incarnations as there are cooks. It's made with beans and without beans; with ground meat and with cubed meat; with beef, pork, poultry or completely vegetarian. If you don't happen to be a chili purist, it's all good.

CHAMPAGNE-
POACHED PEAR
SALAD

Champagne-Poached Pear Salad

Dried cranberries and toasted walnuts add color and crunch to this elegant fruit salad. Right before serving, a golden-brown rectangle of warm, gooey-on-the-inside, crisp-coated Brie is plated with the greens and poached pear.

PREP 30 minutes **COOK** 8 minutes **BAKE** 5 minutes **CHILL** 2 hours

- ¼ cup all-purpose flour
- 1 egg white, beaten
- ¼ cup seasoned fine dry bread crumbs
- 8 2x1x¼-inch pieces Brie or Camembert cheese
- 1 cup extra-dry Champagne or apple cider
- ⅓ cup sugar
- ¼ cup water
- ½ teaspoon whole cloves
- ½ teaspoon whole allspice
- 1 inch stick cinnamon
- 1 vanilla bean, halved lengthwise (optional)
- 4 firm, ripe pears, peeled, halved and cored
- 10 cups mesclun or torn romaine
- ⅔ cup dried tart cherries or dried cranberries
- ½ cup broken walnuts, toasted
  Champagne Vinaigrette (recipe follows)

1. Place flour in a shallow dish. Place egg white in another shallow dish. In a third shallow dish, place bread crumbs. Coat Brie pieces with flour; dip in egg white, then in bread crumbs. Place coated pieces on a lightly greased baking sheet. Place in freezer until needed.

2. In a large skillet, combine Champagne, sugar, the water, cloves, allspice, stick cinnamon and vanilla bean, if you like. Bring to boiling over medium heat, stirring to dissolve sugar; reduce heat. Carefully add pear halves to skillet, cover, and simmer for 8 to 10 minutes or just until pears are tender. (Test for doneness by inserting a wooden toothpick into the thickest part of a pear. The pears should still be slightly firm, but the wooden pick should penetrate easily.) Remove from heat. Drain pears, discarding liquid and spices. Transfer to a bowl. Cover and chill in the refrigerator for 2 hours or until chilled.

3. To serve salad, in a large bowl, combine mesclun, half of the cherries and half of the toasted walnuts. Pour half of the dressing over salad mixture; toss lightly to coat. Set aside. Remove baking sheet from freezer. Bake Brie in a 425° oven for 5 to 6 minutes or until cheese is softened, slightly bubbly and golden brown. Place a pear half and a cheese piece on each salad plate. Place some of the dressed mesclun in the center of each plate. On each serving, drizzle a little more vinaigrette and sprinkle with remaining cherries and walnuts.
Makes 8 servings.

Champagne Vinaigrette: In a screw-top jar, combine ¼ cup champagne vinegar or white wine vinegar, ¼ cup olive oil, 1 tablespoon finely chopped shallot, ¼ teaspoon salt and ⅛ teaspoon freshly ground black pepper. Cover and shake well. Serve immediately or cover and store in refrigerator for up to 1 week. Shake before serving. Makes ½ cup.

Per serving: 306 cal, 14 g fat, 6 mg chol, 216 mg sodium, 38 g carbo, 4 g fiber, 6 g pro.

Wilted Spinach Salad with Hot Bacon Dressing

START TO FINISH 25 minutes

- 8 cups torn fresh spinach (10 ounces) or 6 cups torn fresh spinach and 2 cups torn fresh sorrel
- 1½ cups sliced fresh mushrooms
- 5 slices bacon, cut into 1-inch pieces
- ½ cup chopped onion, finely sliced leek or green onions
- 2 cloves garlic, minced
- ¼ cup white vinegar
- 1 tablespoon sugar
- ½ teaspoon beef bouillon granules
- ¼ teaspoon freshly ground black pepper
- 1 hard-cooked egg, chopped

1. For salad, in a large salad bowl, combine spinach and mushrooms; set aside.

2. For dressing: In a very large skillet, cook bacon over medium heat until crisp. Using a slotted spoon, remove bacon, reserving 2 tablespoons drippings in skillet (add olive oil, if necessary, to measure 2 tablespoons). Drain bacon on paper towels; set aside.

3. Add onion and garlic. Cook and stir over medium-low heat until tender but not brown. Stir vinegar, sugar, bouillon granules and black pepper into the drippings. Bring to boiling; remove from heat. Add the spinach mixture. Toss mixture in the skillet for 30 to 60 seconds or until spinach just starts to wilt.

4. Transfer mixture to salad bowl or individual plates. Sprinkle with bacon and chopped egg. Serve immediately. **Makes 4 to 6 servings.**

Per serving: 179 cal, 13 g fat, 67 mg chol, 320 mg sodium, 9 g carbo, 2 g fiber, 8 g pro.

Holiday Cauliflower

Cauliflower in a creamy Swiss cheese sauce flecked with green sweet pepper and red pimiento provides a little side-dish color on the holiday table.

PREP 25 minutes **BAKE** 15 minutes

    6 cups water
    6 cups cauliflower flowerets (1 large head)
    1 4-ounce can sliced mushrooms, drained
    ¼ cup chopped green sweet pepper
    ¼ cup butter
    ⅓ cup all-purpose flour
    ¼ teaspoon salt
    2 cups milk
    1 cup shredded Swiss cheese (4 ounces)
    2 tablespoons diced pimiento

1. In a large saucepan, bring the water to boiling. Add cauliflower and cook for 4 to 6 minutes or until crisp-tender. Drain cauliflower and set aside.

2. In another saucepan, cook mushrooms and green sweet pepper in butter until pepper is tender. Stir in flour and salt. Add the milk all at once. Cook and stir until bubbly. Remove from heat. Stir in Swiss cheese and pimiento until cheese is melted.

3. In a 1½-quart casserole, place half of the cauliflower. Cover with half of the sauce. Top with remaining cauliflower and sauce.

4. Bake, uncovered, in a 325° oven for 15 minutes. **Makes 8 servings.**

Per serving: 172 cal, 11 g fat, 33 mg chol, 257 mg sodium, 11 g carbo, 3 g fiber, 9 g pro.

Roasted Root Vegetables

PREP 25 minutes **ROAST** 35 minutes

    4 medium parsnips, peeled, halved
       lengthwise and cut into 1-inch pieces
    4 medium turnips, peeled and cut into
       1-inch pieces, or 1 medium rutabaga,
       peeled and cut into 1-inch pieces
    2 small Yukon gold potatoes, peeled and
       cut into quarters, or 1 medium sweet
       potato, peeled and cut into 1-inch pieces
    3 medium carrots, halved lengthwise and
       cut into 1-inch pieces
    2 medium yellow onions, cut into 1-inch-
       wide wedges
    8 leaves of fresh sage, slivered
    3 tablespoons olive oil
    1½ teaspoons sea salt or kosher salt
    ½ teaspoon freshly ground black pepper
    ¼ cup honey
    2 leaves fresh sage

1. In a large greased roasting pan, combine parsnips, turnips, potatoes, carrots, onions, and the eight leaves of slivered sage. Combine oil, salt and pepper; drizzle over vegetables in pan. Toss lightly to coat.

2. Roast, uncovered, in a 425° oven for 30 to 35 minutes until vegetables are lightly browned and tender, stirring occasionally. Drizzle honey over vegetables. Stir gently to coat. Bake 5 minutes more. To serve, sprinkle with the snipped sage. **Makes 8 servings.**

Per serving: 168 cal, 5 g fat, 0 mg chol, 354 mg sodium, 30 g carbo, 5 g fiber, 2 g pro.

While the beef roast, turkey, chicken or ham may garner the most attention and thought, it's the side dishes that round out a memorable and special meal.

ROASTED ROOT
VEGETABLES

Cranberry-Apple Corn Bread Stuffing

If you make your own corn bread, be sure to make it the day before you plan to make the stuffing. Allowing it to dry out just a little bit improves the texture of the finished stuffing.

PREP 35 minutes **BAKE** 50 minutes

½ cup butter

3 medium celery stalks (with leaves), chopped (1½ cups)

1 large yellow onion, chopped (1 cup)

6 cups crumbled corn bread or 6 cups corn bread stuffing mix (two 8-ounce packages)

6 cups dry white or wheat bread cubes

2 cups chopped unpeeled Granny Smith apples

1 cup dried cranberries, cherries or raisins

2 tablespoons snipped fresh sage leaves or 1½ teaspoons dried sage leaves

1 tablespoon snipped fresh thyme leaves or 1 teaspoon dried thyme leaves

½ teaspoon salt

½ teaspoon ground black pepper

1¾ to 2 cups chicken broth (if using stuffing mix, use 3 to 3¼ cups broth)

1. In a large Dutch oven, cook and stir celery and onion in hot butter over medium heat about 5 minutes or until tender. Remove from heat.

2. Stir corn bread, bread cubes, apples, cranberries, sage, thyme, salt and pepper into onion mixture. Drizzle with enough broth to moisten, tossing lightly to combine.

3. Spoon stuffing into a 3-quart baking dish (13x9x2-inch). Bake, covered, in a 325° oven for 35 minutes. Uncover; bake for 15 to 20 minutes more or until heated through and to desired moistness. **Makes 12 to 14 servings.**

Per serving: 293 cal, 14 g fat, 49 mg chol, 648 mg sodium, 37 g carbo, 3 g fiber, 5 g pro.

Many Midwestern towns make the most of Heartland winters during the holidays, when the sparkling white snow provides a backdrop for festive trimmings. The town of St. Charles, Missouri, provides businesses with 10,000 feet of fresh evergreen garlands.

When you're bundled up, letting the snow-kissed landscape take center stage is a great way to celebrate the season. What's better than a pair of fuzzy mittens to keep warm during a day of outside winter play? How about taking a break from sledding to nosh on iced sugar cookie mittens?

Old-Fashioned Buttermilk-Coconut Pie

PREP 25 minutes **BAKE** 52 minutes **COOL** 1 hour

½ of a 15-ounce package rolled refrigerated
 unbaked piecrust (1 crust)
½ cup butter
1¼ cups sugar
¼ cup all-purpose flour
 3 eggs
¾ cup buttermilk
 1 teaspoon vanilla
 1 cup flaked coconut

1. Let piecrust stand according to package directions. Unroll piecrust; place into a 9-inch pie plate. Tuck piecrust edge under and flute edges. Do not prick piecrust. Line pastry with double thickness of foil.

2. Bake in a 450° oven for 8 minutes. Remove foil. Bake for 4 to 6 minutes more or until crust is light brown. Remove from oven. Cool on a wire rack. Reduce oven temperature to 350°.

3. In medium saucepan, melt butter over medium-low heat. Stir in sugar and flour. Remove from heat; set aside.

4. For filling: In a medium bowl, beat eggs lightly with a whisk until combined. Add buttermilk and vanilla; whisk until just combined. Gradually whisk buttermilk mixture into butter mixture until smooth. Stir in coconut.

5. Place partially baked pastry shell on the oven rack. Carefully pour filling into shell. Cover edge of pie with foil to prevent overbrowning.

6. Bake in the 350° oven for 30 minutes. Remove the foil; bake pie about 10 minutes more or until a knife inserted near center comes out clean. Cool slightly on a wire rack. Serve warm. Cover and store any remaining pie in the refrigerator within 2 hours. Let chilled pie stand at room temperature for 1 hour before serving.
Makes 8 servings.

Per serving: 464 cal, 26 g fat, 113 mg chol, 281 mg sodium, 55 g carbo, 1 g fiber, 5 g pro.

Buttermilk-coconut pie and black-bottom pie are both Southern specialties, but really good pie knows no geographic borders. Holiday shoppers in St. Charles, Missouri, stop by Miss Aimee B's Tea Room for a fortifying wedge.

Black-Bottom Pecan Pie

PREP 30 minutes **BAKE** 1 hour

½ of a 15-ounce package rolled refrigerated
 unbaked piecrust (1 crust)
 3 tablespoons butter, softened
¾ cup sugar
¼ cup unsweetened cocoa powder
¼ teaspoon salt
 2 eggs
½ teaspoon vanilla
 2 eggs
½ cup sugar
½ cup light-color corn syrup
 1 tablespoon all-purpose flour
 1 tablespoon butter or margarine, melted
 1 teaspoon vanilla
 1 cup pecan halves

1. Let piecrust stand according to package directions. Unroll piecrust; place into a 9-inch pie plate. Fold piecrust under and flute edges.

2. In a medium bowl, beat the 3 tablespoons butter with an electric mixer on medium to high speed for 30 seconds. Add the ¾ cup sugar, the cocoa powder and salt. Beat until combined, scraping sides of bowl. Beat in the two eggs and ½ teaspoon vanilla until combined. Pour filling into crust. Cover edge of pie with foil to prevent overbrowning.

3. Bake in a 350° oven for 20 minutes or until top of filling is set. Remove pie from oven.

4. In a bowl, lightly beat the two eggs with a fork. Stir in the ½ cup sugar, corn syrup, flour, 1 tablespoon melted butter and 1 teaspoon vanilla; mix well. Stir in the pecans.

5. Carefully spoon topping over filling. Return pie to oven. Bake for 25 minutes. Remove foil. Bake for 15 to 20 minutes more or until a knife inserted near the center comes out clean. Cool on a wire rack. Cover and chill within 2 hours. **Makes 8 servings.**

Per serving: 464 cal, 25 g fat, 123 mg chol, 264 mg sodium, 57 g carbo, 2 g fiber, 6 g pro.

BLACK-BOTTOM
PECAN PIE and
OLD-FASHIONED
BUTTERMILK-
COCONUT PIE

Very Ginger Pound Cake

A topping of kumquats and blood oranges glistening in sugar-sweetened syrup adds sumptuous color to this Christmas cake.

PREP 1 hour **BAKE** 1 hour **STAND** 30 minutes **COOL** 2 hours

5 eggs
1 cup butter
1 cup milk
3 cups all-purpose flour
1 teaspoon baking powder
¼ teaspoon baking soda
¼ teaspoon salt
2 cups granulated sugar
¾ cup packed brown sugar
2 tablespoons grated fresh ginger
2 teaspoons vanilla
½ cup finely chopped crystallized ginger
Blood Orange Topping (recipe follows)

1. Allow eggs, butter and milk to stand at room temperature for 30 minutes. Grease and lightly flour a 10-inch tube pan. In a large bowl, stir together flour, baking powder, baking soda, and salt; set aside.

2. In an extra-large mixing bowl, beat butter with an electric mixer on medium to high speed for 30 seconds. Gradually add granulated sugar and brown sugar, beating until combined. Beat in ginger and vanilla. Add eggs, one at a time, beating for 1 minute after each addition and scraping sides of bowl frequently.

3. Alternately add flour mixture and milk to butter mixture, beating on low to medium speed after each addition just until combined. Gently stir in crystallized ginger. Pour batter into prepared pan.

4. Bake in 350° oven for 60 to 70 minutes or until a cake tester or toothpick inserted near the center comes out clean. Cool in pan on a wire rack for 10 minutes. Remove cake from pan. Cool completely on rack.

5. Meanwhile, prepare Blood Orange Topping.

6. To serve, place cake on a cake stand or serving plate. Gently spoon the fruit in the topping over cake. Drizzle cake and fruit with remaining Blood Orange Topping. **Makes 16 servings.**

Blood Orange Topping: In a medium saucepan, combine 1½ cups granulated sugar and 1 cup water. Bring to boiling; reduce heat. Boil gently, uncovered, for 15 to 20 minutes or until mixture forms a thick syrup, stirring occasionally. Stir more often as syrup begins to thicken (you should have about 1 cup). Meanwhile, thinly slice 3 blood oranges or oranges and 12 kumquats; discard ends and any seeds. Add fruit to syrup, stirring to coat. Return to boiling; reduce heat. Simmer, uncovered, about 5 minutes more or just until fruit is tender, gently turning fruit in syrup several times. Using a slotted spoon, gently remove fruit from syrup. Continue to boil syrup, uncovered, for 10 to 15 minutes more or until syrup is reduced to about ¾ cup. Cool about 15 minutes.

Make-ahead tip: Prepare and bake cake as directed; cool (do not add Blood Orange Topping). Wrap cake in moistureproof and vaporproof wrap or place in an airtight container. Store at room temperature for up to 2 days or freeze for up to 3 months. Thaw wrapped cake at room temperature for several hours. Prepare Blood Orange Topping; spoon topping over cake before serving.

Per serving: 455 cal, 14 g fat, 100 mg chol, 239 mg sodium, 79 g carbo, 2 g fiber, 5 g pro.

Coconut Balls

PREP 10 minutes **BAKE** 12 minutes per batch

- 1 7-ounce package flaked coconut (2⅔ cups)
- 2 tablespoons cornstarch
- ½ cup sweetened condensed milk
- 1 teaspoon vanilla
- ½ cup dried cranberries, snipped dried cherries or chopped dried apricots (optional)

1. Line a large cookie sheet with parchment paper; set aside.

2. In a medium mixing bowl, combine coconut and cornstarch. Stir in sweetened condensed milk and vanilla. Stir in dried fruit, if you like.

3. Drop by small rounded teaspoonfuls about 1 inch apart on the prepared cookie sheets.

4. Bake in a 325° oven for 12 to 15 minutes or until lightly browned on bottoms. Cool on cookie sheet for 1 minute. Transfer cookies to a wire rack; cool. **Makes about 24 cookies.**

Per cookie: 70 cal, 3 g fat, 2 mg chol, 30 mg sodium, 9 g carbo, 1 g fiber, 1 g pro.

Sparkling Sour Cream Sugar Cookies

Lemon extract and orange peel add a citrus touch to these cutout cookies. Top with Powdered Sugar Icing or your favorite frosting before decorating with sprinkles or sanding sugar to make them really shine.

PREP 45 minutes **CHILL** 1 hour **BAKE** 6 minutes per batch

- ½ cup butter, softened
- 1 cup granulated sugar
- 1 teaspoon baking powder
- ¼ teaspoon baking soda
  Dash of salt
- ½ cup dairy sour cream
- 1 egg
- 1 teaspoon finely shredded orange peel
- ½ teaspoon lemon extract
- 2½ cups all-purpose flour
  Powdered Sugar Icing (recipe follows) or your favorite frosting
  Powdered sugar, decorative sprinkles or sanding sugar

1. In a large mixing bowl, beat butter with electric mixer for 30 seconds. Add sugar, baking powder, soda and salt; beat well. Beat in sour cream, egg, orange peel and lemon extract.

2. Beat in as much of the flour as you can with the mixer. Using wooden spoon, stir in the remaining flour. Divide in half. Cover; chill 1 to 2 hours or until easy to handle.

3. On a well-floured surface, roll out half of the dough at a time to ¼-inch thickness. Using a cooking cutter, cut dough into desired shapes. Place cookies 1 inch apart on an ungreased cookie sheet.

4. Bake in a 375° oven for 6 to 7 minutes or until edges are firm and bottoms are light brown. Transfer to wire rack; cool.

5. Prepare the Powdered Sugar Icing or frosting. Spread the icing on cookies. Immediately top each cookie with powdered sugar. **Makes 40 to 50 cookies.**

Powdered Sugar Icing: In a medium mixing bowl, beat together 4 cups sifted powdered sugar and ¼ cup milk. Stir in additional milk if needed, 1 teaspoon at a time, until glaze is easy to spread. Tint with food coloring, if you like.

Per cookie: 105 cal, 3 g fat, 13 mg chol, 50 mg sodium, 18 g carbo, 0 g fiber, 1 g pro.

SPARKLING SOUR
CREAM SUGAR
COOKIES

Orange-Ginger Cookie Sandwiches

These very special cookies are a little fussy to make but worth the effort. Make the Orange Curd filling up to 3 days before using it to streamline the process a bit.

PREP 45 minutes **CHILL** 2 hours **BAKE** 8 minutes per batch

¾ cup whole blanched almonds, toasted
2⅓ cups all-purpose flour
2 teaspoons ground ginger
¾ teaspoon baking soda
¾ teaspoon ground cinnamon
¼ teaspoon salt
¼ teaspoon freshly grated nutmeg or ground nutmeg
⅛ teaspoon ground cloves
1 cup butter, softened
¾ cup granulated sugar
1 egg
2 tablespoons molasses
1 teaspoon finely shredded orange peel
Orange Curd (recipe follows)

1. In a food processor, pulse toasted almonds with on/off turns until finely ground. In a medium bowl, combine flour, the ground almonds, ginger, baking soda, cinnamon, salt, nutmeg and cloves; set aside.

2. In a large bowl, beat butter and granulated sugar with an electric mixer on medium speed until light and fluffy. Add egg, molasses and orange peel. Beat until combined, scraping sides of bowl occasionally. Beat in as much of the flour mixture as you can with the mixer. Using a wooden spoon, stir in any remaining flour mixture. Divide dough in half. Cover and chill for 2 hours or until dough is easy to handle.

3. On a lightly floured surface, roll half of the dough at a time until it is ⅛ to ¼ inch thick. Cut dough using a 2-inch cookie cutter with scalloped edges. Use a metal spatula to place cutouts 1 inch apart on a parchment paper-lined cookie sheet. Using a ¾-inch cookie cutter, cut desired shapes from centers of half of the cookies. Reroll scraps as necessary (if needed, chill scraps before rerolling).

4. Bake cutouts in a 350° oven for 8 to 10 minutes or until edges are light brown. Cool on cookie sheets for 1 minute. Transfer to a wire cooling rack; cool completely.

5. Spread about 1 teaspoon of Orange Curd over the bottom sides of the cookies with no cutouts. Top with the cookies with centers cut out, bottom sides down. Serve within 2 hours. **Makes about 48 sandwich cookies.**

Per cookie: 87 cal, 5 g fat, 15 mg chol, 62 mg sodium, 9 g carbo, 0 g fiber, 1 g pro.

Orange Curd: In a medium saucepan, stir together ¾ cup sugar and 2 tablespoons cornstarch. Add 1 tablespoon finely shredded orange peel and ¾ cup orange juice. Cook and stir over medium heat until thickened and bubbly. Gradually stir about half of the orange mixture into 6 lightly beaten egg yolks. Return egg mixture to saucepan. Cook and stir over medium heat until mixture comes to a gentle boil. Cook and stir for 2 minutes more. Remove from heat. Stir in ½ cup butter, cut up, until butter melts. Transfer to a bowl. Cover surface with plastic wrap. Chill for at least 1 hour. To store, place the prepared curd in an airtight container; cover. Store in the refrigerator for up to 3 days. Makes 1½ cups.

Pecan Butter Balls

PREP 30 minutes **BAKE** 15 minutes per batch

  2 cups finely chopped pecans
  2 cups all-purpose flour
  ½ cup granulated sugar
  ¼ teaspoon salt
  1 cup butter, melted
  2 teaspoons vanilla
1½ cups powdered sugar

1. In a large bowl, combine pecans, flour, granulated sugar and salt; add butter and vanilla. Mix well; shape into a ball. With floured hands, shape into about 1-inch balls. Place 2 inches apart on ungreased cookie sheets.

2. Bake in a 325° oven for 15 to 20 minutes or until bottoms are lightly browned. Cool slightly on a wire rack.

3. Place powdered sugar in a large plastic bag. Add slightly warm cookies in batches to bag. Gently shake to coat. Return to wire rack. Repeat coating with powdered sugar when completely cool. **Makes about 60 cookies.**

Per cookie: 86 cal, 6 g fat, 8 mg chol, 32 mg sodium, 8 g carbo, 0 g fiber, 1 g pro.

Fanciful Peppermint Fudge

PREP 10 minutes **COOK** 10 minutes **CHILL** 4 hours

     Butter
  4 cups granulated sugar
  2 5-ounce cans evaporated milk (1⅓ cups)
  1 cup butter
  1 12-ounce package semisweet chocolate
     pieces (2 cups)
  1 7-ounce jar marshmallow crème
  ½ teaspoon peppermint extract
  ¾ cup coarsely broken peppermint candies*
     (optional)

1. Line a 13x9x2-inch pan with foil, extending foil over edges of pan. Butter foil and set pan aside.

2. Butter the sides of a heavy 3-quart saucepan. In the saucepan, combine the sugar, evaporated milk and the 1 cup butter. Cook and stir over medium-high heat until mixture boils. Reduce heat to medium; continue cooking and stirring 10 minutes.

3. Remove pan from heat. Add chocolate pieces, the marshmallow crème and peppermint extract. Stir until chocolate melts and mixture is combined. Beat by hand for 1 minute. Spread into prepared pan. Sprinkle with peppermint candies, if you like. Score into 1-inch pieces while warm. Cover and chill the fudge.

4. When fudge is firm, use foil to lift it out of the pan. Cut into squares. Store in a tightly covered container in the refrigerator. **Makes 96 (1 piece) servings.**

*Note: For a neat appearance, shake the peppermint pieces in a sieve to remove the very small pieces.

Per serving: 83 cal, 3 g fat, 6 mg chol, 26 mg sodium, 14 g carbo, 0 g fiber, 0 g pro.

A prettily packaged box of homemade candy and cookies is one of the most heartfelt gifts you can give during the busiest season of the year. It's a gift of your time, sweetened with a little bit of sugar.

FANCIFUL
PEPPERMINT FUDGE

Almond Toffee

PREP 25 minutes **COOK** 12 minutes
COOL 4 minutes **STAND** 3 hours

1 cup butter*
1 tablespoon water
1 cup sugar
¾ cup finely chopped toasted almonds
4 to 5 ounces milk chocolate, coarsely
    chopped

1. Line a 13x9x2 baking pan with foil, extending foil over edges. Butter pan.

2. In a heavy 2-quart saucepan, cook butter and the water over high heat to boiling. Add sugar. Reduce heat to medium; cook and stir until sugar is dissolved. Clip candy thermometer to side of pan. Continue cooking, stirring frequently, until thermometer registers 295° (hard-crack stage). Remove from heat. Remove thermometer. Stir in ½ cup of the almonds.

3. Quickly pour candy into prepared pan; spread quickly and evenly. Slide foil and candy out of pan and onto countertop. Cover candy, using Topping Method I or II. **Makes 1¼ pounds candy.**

Topping Method I: Sprinkle chopped chocolate over the top of the hot candy. When it's melted, spread chocolate over the candy. Sprinkle with remaining almonds. Cool candy; break into approximately 24 pieces.

Topping Method II: Score candy into 2x2-inch pieces. Cut and separate pieces; cool until firm. Melt chocolate; spread on tops of pieces. Sprinkle with remaining almonds.

*Note: Be sure to use real butter. With margarine, the fat separates out onto the candy's surface.

Per ⅞-ounce serving: 142 cal, 11 g fat, 21 mg chol, 71 mg sodium, 12 g carbo, 1 g fiber, 1 g pro.

Chocolate Chip Bread Pudding

PREP 20 minutes **BAKE** 50 minutes
COOL 1 hour

6 cups dry firm white bread cubes or dry
    French bread cubes
1¼ cups semisweet chocolate pieces
1 cup coarsely chopped pecans, walnuts or
    almonds
4 eggs
3 cups milk
1 cup sugar
1 tablespoon vanilla
    Brown-Sugar Sauce (recipe follows)

1. Place dry bread cubes in the bottom of a well-buttered 13x9x2-inch baking dish (3-quart rectangular). Sprinkle the chocolate and pecans over dry bread cubes and set aside.

2. In a large mixing bowl, beat together eggs, milk, sugar and vanilla. Pour egg mixture over the bread, the chocolate pieces and the nuts. Gently press down on the bread cubes with the back of a large spoon, making sure the bread absorbs the egg mixture, and the chocolate pieces and nuts are covered with the egg mixture.

3. Bake, uncovered, in a 350° oven for 50 to 60 minutes or until a knife inserted near the center comes out clean. If the top starts to over-brown, cover loosely with foil until custard is set. Cool the bread pudding slightly. Serve warm with Brown-Sugar Sauce. **Makes 12 servings.**

Brown-Sugar Sauce: In a small heavy saucepan, stir together 1 cup packed brown sugar and 2 tablespoons cornstarch. Stir in ½ cup water. Add ⅔ cup half-and-half or light cream, ¼ cup light-color corn syrup and 2 tablespoons butter. Cook and stir over medium heat until bubbly (mixture may look curdled). Cook and stir for 2 minutes more. Remove from heat and stir in 1 teaspoon vanilla. Serve warm over bread pudding. (Cover and chill any leftover sauce for up to 3 days.) Makes 1½ cups sauce.

Per serving: 441 cal, 18 g fat, 86 mg chol, 208 mg sodium, 67 g carbo, 0 g fiber, 9 g pro.

Chocolate-Caramel Fondue

PREP 15 minutes **COOK** 2½ hours to 3 hours on low or 1½ hours on high

1 14-ounce can sweetened condensed milk
1 12-ounce jar caramel ice cream topping
9 ounces semisweet chocolate, coarsely
    chopped, or 1½ cups semisweet
    chocolate pieces
    Assorted dippers (such as angel food
    cake cubes, pound cake cubes, brownie
    squares, cut up salted nut rolls,
    large marshmallows, dried apricots,
    strawberries, banana slices, purchased
    cookies and/or pineapple chunks)
    Milk

1. In a 1½-quart slow cooker, stir together sweetened condensed milk, ice cream topping and chocolate.

2. Cover and cook on low-heat setting for 2½ to 3 hours or on high-heat setting for 1½ hours, stirring once halfway through cooking. If no heat setting is available, cook for 1½ hours. Stir until chocolate is melted. Serve immediately or keep warm in the cooker on low-heat setting (if available) for up to 1 hour. (Chocolate mixture may become grainy if held longer.)

3. To serve, spear dippers with fondue forks. Dip into chocolate mixture, swirling to coat. If the mixture thickens, stir in milk to thin. **Makes 12 servings.**

Per serving: 295 cal, 10 g fat, 11 mg chol, 104 mg sodium, 50 g carbo, 2 g fiber, 6 g pro.

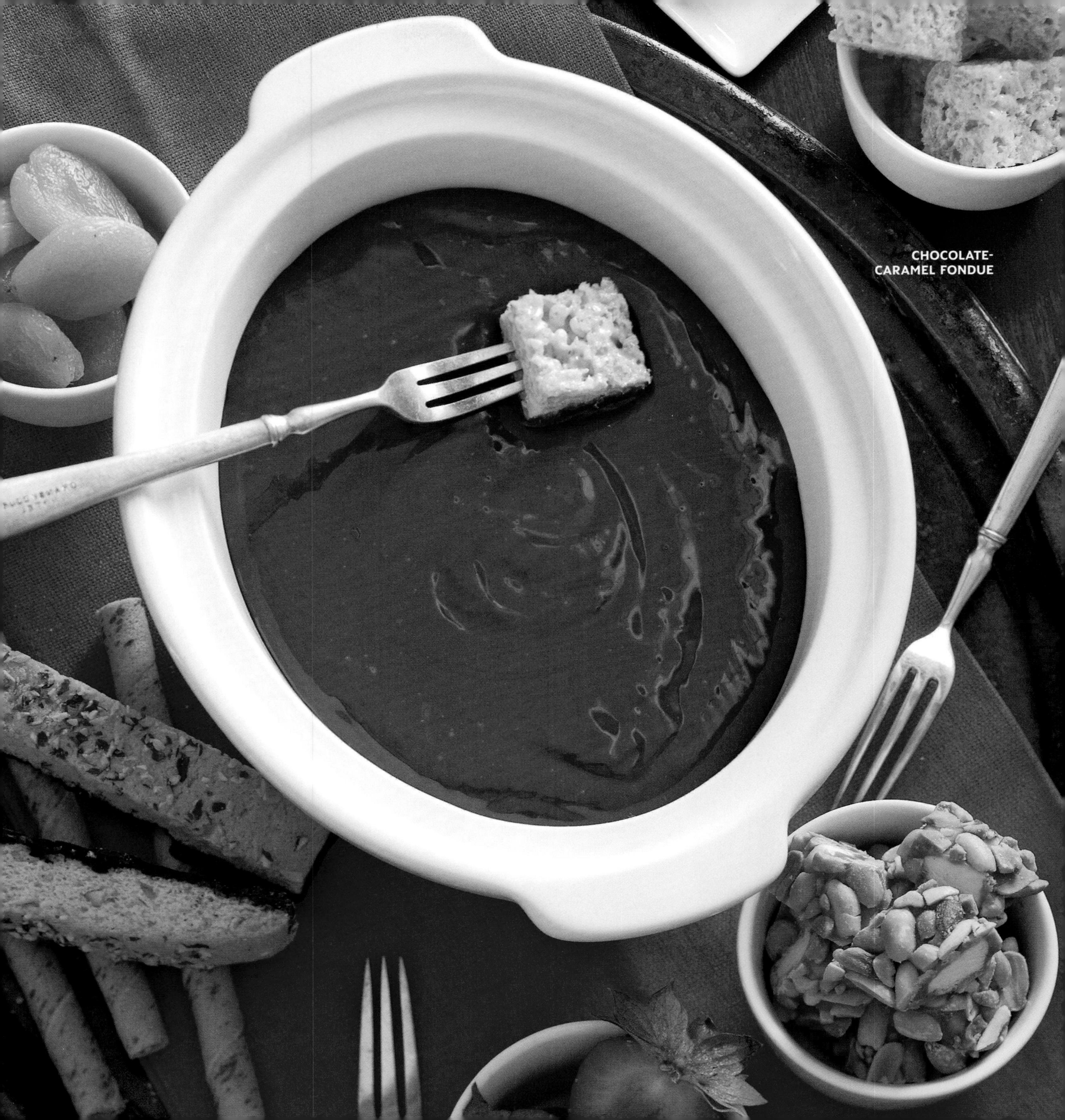

CHOCOLATE-
CARAMEL FONDUE

INDEX

METRIC INFORMATION

The charts on this page provide a guide for converting measurements from the U.S. customary system, which is used throughout this book, to the metric system.

PRODUCT DIFFERENCES

Most of the ingredients called for in the recipes in this book are available in most countries. However, some are known by different names. Here are some common American ingredients and their possible counterparts:

- Sugar (white) is granulated, fine granulated, or castor sugar.
- Confectioners' sugar is icing sugar.
- All-purpose flour is enriched, bleached, or unbleached white household flour. When self-rising flour is used in place of all-purpose flour in a recipe that calls for leavening, omit the leavening agent (baking soda or baking powder) and salt.
- Light-color corn syrup is golden syrup.
- Cornstarch is cornflour.
- Baking soda is bicarbonate of soda.
- Vanilla or vanilla extract is vanilla essence.
- Green, red, or yellow sweet peppers are capsicums or bell peppers.
- Golden raisins are sultanas.

VOLUME AND WEIGHT

The United States traditionally uses cup measures for liquid and solid ingredients. The chart, top right, shows the approximate imperial and metric equivalents. If you are accustomed to weighing solid ingredients, the following approximate equivalents will be helpful.

- 1 cup butter, castor sugar, or rice = 8 ounces = ½ pound = 250 grams
- 1 cup flour = 4 ounces = ¼ pound = 125 grams
- 1 cup icing sugar = 5 ounces = 150 grams

Canadian and U.S. volume for a cup measure is 8 fluid ounces (237 ml), but the standard metric equivalent is 250 ml. 1 British imperial cup is 10 fluid ounces.

In Australia, 1 tablespoon equals 20 ml, and there are 4 teaspoons in the Australian tablespoon.

Spoon measures are used for smaller amounts of ingredients. Although the size of the tablespoon varies slightly in different countries, for practical purposes and for recipes in this book, a straight substitution is all that's necessary. Measurements made using cups or spoons always should be level unless stated otherwise.

COMMON WEIGHT RANGE REPLACEMENTS

Imperial / U.S.	Metric
½ ounce	15 g
1 ounce	25 g or 30 g
4 ounces (¼ pound)	115 g or 125 g
8 ounces (½ pound)	225 g or 250 g
16 ounces (1 pound)	450 g or 500 g
1¼ pounds	625 g
1½ pounds	750 g
2 pounds or 2¼ pounds	1,000 g or 1 Kg

OVEN TEMPERATURE EQUIVALENTS

Fahrenheit Setting	Celsius Setting*	Gas Setting
300°F	150°C	Gas Mark 2 (very low)
325°F	160°C	Gas Mark 3 (low)
350°F	180°C	Gas Mark 4 (moderate)
375°F	190°C	Gas Mark 5 (moderate)
400°F	200°C	Gas Mark 6 (hot)
425°F	220°C	Gas Mark 7 (hot)
450°F	230°C	Gas Mark 8 (very hot)
475°F	240°C	Gas Mark 9 (very hot)
500°F	260°C	Gas Mark 10 (extremely hot)
Broil	Broil	Grill

*Electric and gas ovens may be calibrated using celsius. However, for an electric oven, increase celsius setting 10 to 20 degrees when cooking above 160°C. For convection or forced air ovens (gas or electric) lower the temperature setting 25°F/10°C when cooking at all heat levels.

BAKING PAN SIZES

Imperial / U.S.	Metric
9x1½-inch round cake pan	22- or 23x4-cm (1.5 L)
9x1½-inch pie plate	22- or 23x4-cm (1 L)
8x8x2-inch square cake pan	20x5-cm (2 L)
9x9x2-inch square cake pan	22- or 23x4.5-cm (2.5 L)
11x7x1½-inch baking pan	28x17x4-cm (2 L)
2-quart rectangular baking pan	30x19x4.5-cm (3 L)
13x9x2-inch baking pan	34x22x4.5-cm (3.5 L)
15x10x1-inch jelly roll pan	40x25x2-cm
9x5x3-inch loaf pan	23x13x8-cm (2 L)
2-quart casserole	2 L

U.S. / STANDARD METRIC EQUIVALENTS

⅛ teaspoon = 0.5 ml	⅓ cup = 3 fluid ounces = 75 ml
¼ teaspoon = 1 ml	½ cup = 4 fluid ounces = 125 ml
½ teaspoon = 2 ml	⅔ cup = 5 fluid ounces = 150 ml
1 teaspoon = 5 ml	¾ cup = 6 fluid ounces = 175 ml
1 tablespoon = 15 ml	1 cup = 8 fluid ounces = 250 ml
2 tablespoons = 25 ml	2 cups = 1 pint = 500 ml
¼ cup = 2 fluid ounces = 50 ml	1 quart = 1 litre